The End

of the

Risk-Free
Rate

The End

of the

Risk–Free Rate

Investing When
Structural Forces Change
Government Debt

BEN EMONS

New York Chicago San Francisco Athens London
Madrid Mexico City Milan New Delhi
Singapore Sydney Toronto

2 3 4 5 6 7 8 9 0   DOC/DOC   1 9 8 7 6 5 4 3

ISBN: 978-0-07-181952-7
MHID: 0-07-181952-5

e-ISBN: 978-0-07-181953-4
e-MHID: 0-07-181953-3

This publication is designed to provide accurate and authoritative information in regard to the subject matter covered. It is sold with the understanding that neither the author nor the publisher is engaged in rendering legal, accounting, or other professional service. If legal advice or other expert assistance is required, the services of a competent professional person should be sought.
—*From a Declaration of Principles Jointly Adopted by a Committee of the American Bar Association and a Committee of Publishers and Associations*

The views contained herein are the author's but not necessarily those of PIMCO. Such opinions are subject to change without notice. This publication has been distributed for educational purposes only and should not be considered as investment advice or a recommendation of any particular security, strategy, or investment product. Information contained herein has been obtained from sources believed to be reliable, but not guaranteed.

Nothing contained herein is intended to constitute accounting, legal, tax, securities, or investment advice, nor an opinion regarding the appropriateness of any investment, nor a solicitation of any type. This publication contains a general discussion of economic theory and the investment marketplace, including but not limited to the "risk-free rate" and investment instruments that are generally perceived by the marketplace as "risk free," "safe," or "low risk"; readers should be aware that all investments carry risk and may lose value. The information contained herein should not be acted upon without obtaining specific accounting, legal, tax, and investment advice from a licensed professional.

McGraw-Hill Education books are available at special quantity discounts to use as premiums and sales promotions, or for use in corporate training programs. To contact a representative, please e-mail us at bulksales@mheducation.com.

This book is dedicated to my wife, Buwon, our son, Derek, and our daughter, Ellison, for their love and patience. Special gratitude to my mother-in-law, Huong.

This book is also dedicated to my parents, Han and Jerry, my sister, Annemarie, and my family in the UK and Breda, the Netherlands.

Thanks to friends and family in the Netherlands and Los Angeles, Tony Crescenzi, USC EMBA Class 22, USC friends, and Pacific Investment Management Company.

Contents

A Prelude: Financial Markets Finance

Financial markets are a conglomerate. They represent a mass of different play-ers that express views, have expectations, and take actions. Financial markets are about psychology, about human interaction in a highly technologically advanced environment, where information is a crucial commodity for achieving returns on and return of capital. Financial markets allow companies, governments, and individuals to have access to capital markets for funding of projects, buildings, bridges, retirements, fiscal and current account deficits, credit, housing, political and military campaigns, and much more. Financial markets are a barometer of economic activity and instantly react to worldwide developments. They have been a source of innovation, financial engineering, and product creativity and a provider of employment.

Economists such as Hyman Minsky and John Maynard Keynes have described financial markets as the "casino" of the capitalist economy, whereby players increase their stakes thanks to markets' provision of leverage. Despite increased regulation and efforts to stem excesses that yield severe financial crises such as that in 2008, financial markets are places that have enormous power over societies and economies. In finance theory, the basics are about supply and demand. Financial markets are all about that—the pinnacle of supply and demand for global liquidity. The dynamics of the different markets that make up the entire marketplace; the specifics and intricacies of financial securities and participants who invest in them; the transfer of risk, return, and liquidity; as well as the way developments and financial domino effects impact multiple markets at the same time fall under the definition of "financial markets finance." There is one basic element, a foundation on which much of finance in financial markets is based: "the risk-free rate," or the rate that in theory carries no investment risk. It could be seen as the magic stick to the promised land of wealth; on the other hand, the prices of bonds, stocks, commodities, and currencies all have incorporated the assumption of a risk-free rate. This assumption has been brought into question since the financial crisis. It has been revealed that the risk-free rate is basically no more, although it could be argued that the rate has always been a theoretical concept and that all investments contain some level of risk.

That said, through the ages, countries have relied on the risk-free rate to issue debt. This reliance on debt financing has provided vital resources for societies to grow. Today, many developed countries are engulfed by large public debt loads. Their potential growth rates have shifted lower, and population growth is diminishing. The trajectory of debt relative to gross domestic product is on an unsustainable track and requires significantly negative real and nominal interest rates to maintain financing. This has put the core of financial markets finance in jeopardy, the risk-free rate that is used as input into many models for both fixed income and equity valuation.

This book takes a tour around the different factors that influence the risk-free rate. By no means is the purpose of this book to steer investors away from fixed income. On the contrary, the title "end" of the risk-free rate is meant to provide insight for investors to look at financial markets finance in a different way. This means accepting that the concept of the risk-free rate is something from the past. Things that were once assumed to be risk free, such as Treasury bills and government bonds, have more risk characteristics. There are alternatives in fixed income that investors have been seeking, and there, too, the valuation based off an assumed risk-free rate may have to be questioned. To that extent, this book provides a look at risk premiums and valuations. The end of the risk-free rate does not mean an end to investing, but rather a new step into a different investing world.

Part I

A Different Financial Universe

Chapter 1

No Longer a True Risk-Free Rate

When something is "risk free," it is desired—for example, a free lunch, a coupon, or a ticket to see a popular show. In financial markets, the economic concept of a risk-free rate is quite similar. In times of high uncertainty or distress, market participants want something that has 100 percent probability of being returned to them. The choice is typically cash or what has long been assumed to be a risk-free instrument, a Treasury bill or government bond. Nothing is truly free in financial terms unless there is a full backstop or subsidy of some kind. And so government bonds were viewed that way, boring instruments with a low return because they are public goods. Government bonds have been for a long time in the category of a benchmark for a "safe haven," a beacon of perceived neutrality between risk and return. There has been a change in that definition, known as the "risk-free rate." The onset of the financial crisis saw large guarantees of their financial systems by governments, and as economies fell into a deep recession, automatic stabilizers as well as additional fiscal stimulus increased governments' total debts. What was normally considered as a steady, boring investment has changed to a volatile instrument with credit risk characteristics.

The implications of such a change are vast. Government bonds no longer being truly risk-free may change the way markets and academics view the valuation of risk premiums for equities; corporate, municipal, mortgage, and agency bonds; and even highly complex structured finance such as collateralized loan obligations (CLOs) and collateralized debt obligations (CDOs). Another implication is that governments' balance sheets fall in the rank of how corporate balance sheets are valued. A government balance sheet liability is the interest it pays on its debt. The ability of a government to pay that interest has been put into question by markets over the past few years, especially for certain governments in Europe. It is a confidence crisis in public debt. This is not the first time such a crisis has occurred. Emerging markets have succumbed to the idea of defaulting on their external and internal debt as an easy way out of their economic problems. Other countries, such as Italy in the 1970s, have used large-scale monetization of debt. The result was currency devaluation that caused high domestic inflation, an indirect way of default. The rules of default and restructuring were never clearly defined until the Argentina 2001 debt default happened. The rules laid out in so-called Collective Action Clauses (CACs) by the G7 working group are now mainstream in Europe. This could drastically alter the way markets will price the probability of default or how a sovereign restructuring ultimately unfolds. The first test has happened in Greece in 2012. Greek government bonds that were issued with CACs turned out to be more complicated to restructure than bonds without CACs. This was specifically because of the right of investors to disagree with the new terms on their bonds through majority voting. Democracy in future debt restructurings may cause dilemmas for governments and policymakers. In a financial world that no longer operates on the basis of a risk-free rate, the health of the financial sector and governments has a close interconnection. There is an inherent linkage between sovereign and financial risks, and the European debt crisis has shown that such a linkage presents channels of cross-border spillovers. The experience encourages proactive policies to manage sovereign risk to safeguard financial stability. To that effect, measures are needed to stabilize the banking sector. Done effectively, this can have a favorable impact on sovereign balance sheets. As the notion of risk free has changed, countries with large potential liabilities from their banking sectors will be continuously scrutinized by markets, which will assess if there is a framework in place that identifies, monitors, and reports related risks closely. A government bond market has a crucial role in how a society can function. Government bonds provide funding for education, healthcare, law enforcement, and other public goods. The inability to access capital markets will affect basic public services and can adversely affect the economy.

The Risk-Free Rate in Theory

Michael Schmidt (a columnist for Investopedia) analyzed the risk-free rate of return as one of the most basic elements of modern finance. Many of its most famous theories—the capital asset pricing model (CAPM), modern portfolio theory (MPT), and the Black-Scholes model—use the risk-free rate as the primary component from which other valuations are derived. The risk-free asset applies only in theory, but its actual safety rarely comes into question until events fall far beyond the normal daily market volatility. Although it is easy to take shots at theories that have a risk-free asset as their base, there are limited options to use as a proxy. The risk-free rate is an important building block for MPT, which assumes there is one risk-free rate. The risk-free asset is the (hypothetical) asset that pays a "low" rate. The risk-free asset has zero variance in returns and is also uncorrelated with any other asset. As a result, when it is combined with any other asset or portfolio of assets, the change in return is linearly related to the change in risk as the proportions in the combination vary. MPT uses the risk-free rate as a starting point to determine the "optimum" portfolio on the efficient frontier, the set of combinations

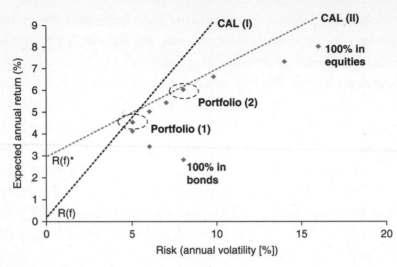

Figure 1.1   Expected return versus risk.

of assets' expected returns and volatility. The formula is used to calculate the expected return that represents the capital allocation line,
a measure of the risk of risky and risk-free assets, where the slope is
known as the "reward-to-variability ratio." The risk-free rate is an
important attribution factor because it determines the slope of the line,
which can determine the tangent portfolio (optimum portfolio) on the
efficient frontier. MPT never assumed a change in the risk-free rate,
simply because it was viewed as the prevailing level of interest rates
on government bonds at a certain point in time. If the risk-free rate
has changed in terms of risk characteristics, it would also challenge the
slope of the capital asset allocation line and thereby the selection of the
optimum portfolio. To prove this in a simple exercise, Figure 1.1 shows
two risk-free rates, "R(f)" at 0.25 percent and "R(f)*" at 3 percent. R(f)
represents the level of the risk-free rate where most central bank rates
are near zero, which has impacted money market rates and short-term
government bonds trading at similar levels. R(f)* is the new risk-free
rate, at a higher level because a risk premium has been added to R(f).
In Figure 1.1, this has an immediate result. The capital asset allocation

line, "CAL (I)," shifts out to "CAL(II)," which changes the optimal portfolio (1) to portfolio (2) on the efficient frontier. The expected return of the optimal portfolio goes from 4 to 6 percent, but what is notable as a result of a higher risk-free rate is that the annual volatility doubles from 5 to 10 percent. The risk premium of 2.75 percent, the difference between R(f)* and R(f), consists of several components, such as inflation, default, and liquidity, but now also debt, deficit, and political risk.

The term *risk* is often taken for granted and used very loosely, especially when it comes to the risk-free rate. At its most basic level, risk is the probability of events or outcomes. Michael Schmidt shows that when applied to investments, risk can be broken down in a number of ways. There is "absolute risk" as defined by volatility, quantified by common measures such as standard deviation. Because risk-free assets "typically" mature in 3 months or less, the volatility measure is low and short term in nature. There is also the idea of "relative risk." This is risk when applied to investments and is usually represented by the relation of price fluctuations of an asset to an index or base. Lastly, there is "default risk." In this case, it could be the risk the U.S. government would default on its debt obligations. Although the U.S. government has never defaulted on any of its debt obligations, the risk of default has been raised during extreme economic events when the U.S. government has stepped in to provide a level of security that provided a perception of safety. Michael Schmidt argues that the U.S. government can spin the ultimate security of its debt in unlimited ways, but the reality is that the U.S. dollar is no longer backed by gold, so the only true security for its debt is the government's ability to make the payments from current balances or tax revenues. This raises many questions about the reality of a risk-free asset. For example, say the economic environment is such that there is a large deficit being funded by debt and the current administration plans to reduce taxes and provide tax incentives to both individuals and companies to spur economic growth. If this plan were used by a publicly held company, how could the company justify its credit quality if the plan were to basically decrease revenue and increase spending? That in itself has been the rub up until the financial crisis: there was really no justification or alternative for the risk-free asset (source; Michael Schmidt).

There have been attempts to use other options, but the U.S. T-bill remains the best option because it has been the closest investment—in theory and reality—to a short-term riskless security. This idea about the risk-free rate has materially changed since the crisis. Until the crisis of 2008, the risk-free rate was rarely called into question. Reasons why this question is arising today are that the economic environments in developed countries have remained in disarray or catastrophic events have occurred, such as credit market collapses, war, stock market collapses, and currency devaluations. These can all lead people to question the safety and security of a government as a credible borrower. The best way to evaluate the riskless security would be to use standard techniques, such as those to evaluate the creditworthiness of a company. Unfortunately, such metrics applied to a government rarely hold up because a government basically exists in perpetuity by nature and has "unlimited" powers to raise funds in both the short and the long term. A way that the risk-free rate is judged in markets for its level of valuation is by applying the theory of the real rate of interest by Irving Fisher. In his work *The Theory of Interest* (1930), he laid out a thesis that when the rate of inflation is sufficiently low, the real rate of interest can be approximated by the nominal rate minus the rate of inflation, which became known as the "Fisher equation." For inflation to stay low so that the Fisher equation holds, it is necessary that inflation expectations remain stable. By replacing the inflation term in the Fisher equation with inflation expectations, the real rate is based on the nominal rate minus the expected rate of inflation. In other words, the nominal rate can be determined by taking the real rate plus the expected rate of inflation. Why is this relevant for the discussion about the risk-free rate? One aspect that determines the nominal rate of a government bond is inflation expectations. That means the yield also reflects an expectation of a future real rate in order to give the bondholder sufficient return for potential higher inflation down the road. This is called the "interest rate risk component" of the risk-free rate. When inflation rises, investors seek higher nominal interest rates that are above the rate of inflation. Coupled with expectations, the central bank may raise interest rates; higher inflation generally leads to higher interest rates. Since 2009, inflation has been rising in most developed countries from a combination of higher energy prices and large-scale asset purchase programs by central banks that induced inflation expectations. Using the Fisher equation, the nominal risk free rate could be approximated by the sum of the expected real rate and the expected rate of inflation. There is also a "credit component." This is the expectation of default and the ability to continue to borrow. In financial markets, this is distinguished by secured and unsecured borrowing and lending. "Unsecured" refers to higher credit risk because the collateral or promise backing the loan has a higher probability of not being fulfilled. An expression of how high that risk may be is the "swap spread." Interest rate swaps are derivatives contracts in which parties agree to exchange fixed and floating rates for a period of time. These contracts are typically agreed upon between banks and private entities, but at times, government agencies that issue government bonds also use them for hedging purposes. The difference between the swap rate and government bond yield is often seen as a sign of stress or calm in the financial system. To gauge the interest rate risk and credit risk components in short-term interest rates, Figure 1.2 shows both measured in basis points (1/100th of a percent). The interest rate component is the difference between the actual short-term rate and short-term inflation expectations. The other line is the swap spread, the difference between short-term Treasury bond yield and interest rate swap. What is notable is that for the United States, both components have been on the rise since late 2008, when the Federal Reserve Funds rate has been at 0 to 0.25 percent.

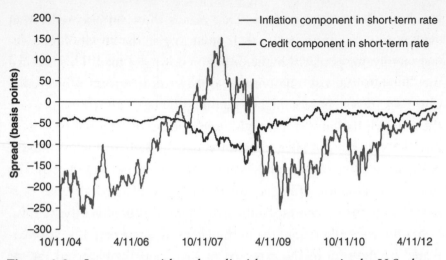

Figure 1.2   Interest rate risk and credit risk components in the U.S. short-term rate. Credit component = difference between T-bill yield and LIBOR. Inflation component = T-bill yield − short-term inflation expectations. (*Source:* Bloomberg.)

No Longer a True Risk-Free Rate

To state it in bold terms, there is no longer a "true" gauge for the risk-free rate. There are several reasons why. For example, Treasury bills have yielded zero or negative returns over the past few years. Even though this may be a sign of safety, as conceivably no or negative return implies no risk, in general, investors reject a negative or zero yield as being investable, either per guidelines or psychologically. As rating agencies downgraded a variety of sovereign issuers, including the United States and the United Kingdom, the universe of AAA-rated government bond issuers has shrunk. The effect of this was dramatic in smaller bond markets. For example, Sweden and Australia saw an increase of foreign ownership of up to 80 percent, according to data of the Swedish and Australian Treasury. Such high ownership has served in crises times as a potential catalyst for sudden capital withdrawal, affecting the value of bonds adversely. Thus, even though the Australian and Swedish governments are AAA, their bond markets are vulnerable to capital withdrawal because foreign investors are likely more easily enticed to do so than domestic investors. There was a flight to quality during 2011 and 2012 stemming from the European debt crisis. This led to large inflows into corporate bonds, specifically those in the United States. The yield on the Barclays BBB-rated corporate bond index fell to a record low of 2.56 percent in 2012, below that of the yield on a 30-year U.S. Treasury bond at some point. This is a reflection of investors' perception of safety, whereby corporations are seen as having a sounder, healthier financial state than the government. That said, a corporate bond is by definition never defined as "risk free" because it is generally lower rated than a government bond, and companies are always vulnerable to the economy, competition, and access to capital markets. As interest rates fell to new lows, the duration of 30-year government bonds has risen to over 20 years, producing more risks—interest rate, credit, and inflation—for fewer yields. To the same degree, thanks to quantitative easing, U.S. mortgage-backed securities by Fannie Mae and Freddie Mac became excessively overvalued relative to their prepayment risk. These examples show that even though interest rates are at record lows and thus perceived to be in demand, there is a mismatch with the underlying fundamental risk. In a different way, the European debt crisis revealed what modern-day sovereign risk is about. European government bond yields became distressed because of a combination of heightened political, economic, and financial risk. Underneath there was a host of risk elements, including sequential rating downgrades, private sector involvement, restructuring, currency convertibility, social-political rejection, and "debt mutualization." These elements are no longer unique to European government bonds, but now extend to all major sovereign bond markets for the simple reason that there is too much government debt outstanding and too little growth to back those liabilities.

Another form of a risk-free rate was the London Interbank Offered Rate, "LIBOR." During the heyday of the structured credit securitization boom of 2002 to 2007, this was regarded as the trusted rate to back approximately $300 trillion notional in derivatives, according to the Bank for International Settlements. LIBOR was a rate that was fixed by a panel of banks each day at 11 AM London time. It also served as a benchmark for interbank lending. By 2006 to 2007, there was a growing suspicion that a number of banks were under- or overstating LIBOR as confidence started to wane in the valuation of mortgage-backed securities and structured credit often referenced to LIBOR. After initial investigations, LIBOR became a "scandal" in 2012, when even the Bank of England monetary policy committee members were questioned in terms of their involvement and oversight. The confidence in LIBOR became so undermined that it resulted in a regulatory overhaul. The result was that LIBOR, embedded in floating rate mortgages, credit derivatives, and short-term interest rate futures, was no longer regarded as a "risk-free rate." It questioned the valuation of many derivatives.

In finance, the risk-free rate is used to calculate expected returns, cost of capital, and net present values. It conceivably no longer being the same calls into question those finance measures and risk premiums in general. All else being equal, the risk-free rate being implicitly higher increases discount rates and reduces the present value of discounted cash flow valuations. Changes in the risk-free rate also have consequences for both equity risk premium and debt because of higher default. Other factors that cause a shift in risk-free rates—expected inflation and real economic growth—can also affect the expected cash flows for a firm, a government, and now a central bank holding large amounts of assets. Thus, even though government bond yields are held artificially low, the starting point for the risk-free rate has shifted. There are different ways to calculate this, such as with debt sustainability formulas. Taking the United States, the United Kingdom, Italy, and Spain as examples displayed in Table 1.1, their 10-year yields are compared with an "equilibrium" yield, a yield needed to stabilize debt to gross domestic product (GDP). The table suggests that yields have to be significantly negative to sustain

Table 1.1   10-Year Yields and Equilibrium Yields*

Country	2012 Year-End Generic 10-Year Yield (%)	Equilibrium 10-Year Yield (%)
United States	1.75	−4.4
United Kingdom	1.82	−5.8
Italy	4.49	−2.7
Spain	5.26	−7.4

*Debt sustainability formula $d(t) = -pb(t) + (1+i-g)*d(t-1)$, where $d(t)$, $d(t-1)$ = current debt/gross domestic product (GDP) projection for 2012; g = growth rate projection for 2012; i = level of nominal 10-year interest rate; and $pb(t)$ = primary balance for 2012. From the debt sustainability formula, you can derive the "equilibrium" interest $(i) = pb(t)/d(t-1)*100+g$. This is the level of interest rate to stabilize the debt/GDP at the level of primary balance and growth. Equilibrium yield for the United States = $(-6.8/107*100) +2 = -4.4$.
(*Source:* Bloomberg; 2012 year-end generic yield levels; IMF Fiscal Monitor, October 2012; IMF World Economic Outlook, October 2012.)

the debt-to-GDP ratio at present levels. Albeit in all four countries, the central bank is committed to either infinite quantitative easing (QE) or provision of liquidity to banks, the yields embed a significant risk premium compared with the equilibrium rate.

In the International Monetary Fund's (IMF's) World Economic Outlook of October 2012—referred to as "the good, the bad, and the ugly"—the research investigates 26 historical cases of countries with debt exceeding 100 percent of GDP. The history offers a few lessons. Without any growth (obviously), fiscal consolidation is futile. Fiscal measures need to be permanent to reduce debt, and even when austerity is followed, it can take an average of 10 years to see results. Low or falling nominal interest rates and inflation were crucial to reducing the debt-to-GDP ratio. Restoring competitiveness only through domestic deflation and reducing debt only through austerity, not inflation, holds back growth for years, and debt ratios may actually rise. This rising debt-to-GDP ratio incrementally adds a risk premium to government bonds over time, a premium that implies higher expectations of default than what has been the case in the past.

In May 2011, the IMF presented a report about what it means to live in a world without a risk-free rate. The IMF concluded that because the health of the financial sector and the government are closely interconnected, a better understanding of the linkages between sovereign issuers and financial risks was needed. Investors needed to conduct a thorough analysis of the channels of cross-border spillovers. In addition, policymakers were required to help manage sovereign risk to create a positive impact on financial stability. They needed to apply measures to stabilize the banking sector to have a favorable impact on sovereign balance sheets. The IMF advised that countries with large potential liabilities from their banking sectors need to identify, monitor, and report related risks closely. There was a clear need for impact analysis of contingent liabilities on the government's financial position. That included a government's overall access to liquidity and an assessment of future borrowing decisions. The exposure of sovereign risks also involved a call for stronger emphasis on stress tests. There was anecdotal evidence that some debt managers were complementing existing analytical approaches with a greater focus on stress scenarios, including extreme financing shocks. Policymakers could take the extra step and contemplate the role of a joint stress test for systemically important financial institutions and sovereigns. The outcomes of such stress tests could help inform crisis preparedness, debt strategies, and financial supervision and regulation.

There are also implications for supply and demand. On the demand side of the market, dealers and investors no longer treat government bonds as purely interest rate products. Far from it— government bonds have assumed characteristics typical of credit products, for which prices mainly provide measures of borrowers' probabilities of default. Many are not as liquid as before, and their investor base is not as diversified as it used to be. During phases of risk aversion, they do not benefit from flight to quality flows. On the contrary, they correlate with riskier assets. Credit rating downgrades play a pro-cyclical role and can exacerbate these adverse dynamics. Central bankers generally accept government bonds as collateral in refinancing operations, but below certain thresholds, lower ratings could trigger sizable haircuts (in other words, revaluing the bonds substantially below their market value). Regulators could also assign them a nonzero risk weight under the standardized approach, so that suddenly these bonds are not risk-free rates any longer. And even if bonds such as U.S. Treasuries and German Bunds have retained most of their risk-free characteristics, the once solid dividing line between interest rate and credit products has become blurred. In the long run, such changes can profoundly affect investors' choices. One example of these changes is that more capital may flow toward emerging markets. These economies have been able to absorb the recent inflows, but the increase in corporate and financial leverage, rising asset prices, and building inflationary pressures may soon translate into growing imbalances and open the door to a new set of challenges to financial stability. On the supply side of the market, debt managers in advanced economies have started behaving a bit like their emerging market colleagues. Given the increased exposure to economic and financial risks, they have started placing stronger emphasis on risk mitigation strategies, well beyond what traditional debt management objectives would indicate. Confronted with the usual trade-off between being predictable and being flexible, most of them have erred on the side of flexibility. While retaining an open dialogue with financial markets, they realize that annual programs have to offer sufficient flexibility to cope with the challenges of issuing and managing larger amounts of debt. Finally, debt managers are putting a high premium on proactive and timely communication as well as on understanding the evolving nature of the investor base. These are precisely the elements that were outlined in the "Stockholm principles" the IMF facilitated with the debt managers in September 2010. The global crisis is sending many back to the drawing board to take a fresh look at old assumptions and long-cherished principles, and the risk-free nature of government bonds is therefore no exception.

Supply and Demand of Risk-Free Rates

The demand for "safe assets" or those assets that are perceived to be safe is on the rise, yet fewer of them are being issued, which is likely to increase the price of safety on financial markets. Each financial asset has intrinsic characteristics, one of which is safety. Other factors at work can be viewed as external. They are regulations, collateral, and central bank operations that can have an effect on the pricing of assets with potential distortions. Before the financial crisis, there was a host of regulations, inflation targeting policies, and lack of "macro prudential" rules that almost openly encouraged the underpricing of safe assets by allowing excessive risk taking. Financial market regulators have forcefully responded to the 2008 crisis, with Basel III and the Volcker rule as prime examples. These measures are against a backdrop of uncertainty that has proven to be stickier than first thought. The forces that cause uncertainty may be structural and thereby have a shrinking effect on the supply of assets that are considered to be "safe," such as government bonds from countries that still enjoy AAA sovereign credit ratings. This may raise the price of safe assets. These assets have a store of value function and are, in the context of portfolios, used to help preserve capital. They are also used as an inventory of liquid and stable collateral used in repurchase ("repo") agreements by banks. They are also important in derivatives markets, where they play a role of trust in financial negotiations.

Increased regulations require banks to enhance capital and liquidity buffers. As the instrument of choice, typically assets such as government bonds are chosen. With monetary policy being active, safe assets became a crucial policy tool in open market operations to influence financial conditions. These widely varying roles of safe assets see differentials across markets in the price of safety. Along comes the complication of a vast amount of different types of market participants that each assign specific attributes to what they see as safety. Whether acting as a store of value, an instrument to hedge contingent liabilities, or a value instrument to buy and hold for the long term, collectively safe assets have a dynamic definition. With increasing market share by central banks and other official sector players, the distortion may pose a challenge to the ability of safe assets to fulfill all roles. Specifically, now that the application of zero risk weight assignment to sovereign debt is no longer a virtue, there is a clear perception that safety is no longer detached from underlying economic risks. The imbalance of supply and demand for safe, risk-free assets was further exaggerated through the financial crisis. The aftermath produced heightened uncertainty in addition to regulatory reforms, and the demand for certain categories of safe, risk-free assets went up. That demand is coming at a time when the universe of what is considered to be safe and risk free is shrinking. Regulatory reforms intended to make institutions more sound cause insufficient differentiation across eligible assets to satisfy regulatory requirements. This has the unintended consequence of a "cliff effect" when risk-free rates are unsafe and thereby unable to satisfy regulatory criteria. In theory, a risk-free rate should have an identical payoff in any market around the world. In practice, risk-free assets are subject to risks. Therefore, when credit rating agencies assign them the highest rating and they are embedded in regulations as well as benchmark guidelines for institutional investors, this may lead to an erroneously high level of perceived safety. Such views may prove to be inaccurate or complacent, thereby exposing institutions and markets to a higher concentration of credit risks. The underpricing of safety has been linked to an over-reliance on credit ratings and the wrong incentives. The financial crisis revealed that it is by no means guaranteed that financial assets are safe, as seen by the massive losses on AAA-rated tranches of mortgage-backed securities or the recent sequential downgrades of European sovereigns.

A historical overview of sovereign debt ratings suggests that shifts in relative safety have precedents. However, the current degree of differentiation across sovereigns in the world is more pronounced than in previous periods, with historically low ratings in southern Europe, Iceland, and Ireland and downgrades in countries that had maintained AAA ratings since S&P reinstated sovereign ratings in the mid-1970s, namely Austria, France, and the United States. Sovereign ratings in Greece, Iceland, Ireland, Italy, Portugal, and Spain had a sharp downward correction after an increase in the 1990s. Government debt issuers were predominantly rated AAA during the 1990s. The share of unrated sovereigns was high until the mid-1980s, in part reflecting low defaults and high perceptions of safety in the 1960s and 1970s. The first three points suggest that during some periods, such as periods of calm, ratings did not sufficiently capture the credit quality of assets with varied underlying fundamentals. In practice, relative asset safety can be seen by considering a continuum of asset characteristics. Safe assets meet the criteria of (1) low credit and market risks, (2) high market liquidity, (3) limited inflation risks, (4) low exchange rate risks, and (5) limited idiosyncratic risks. The first criterion, low credit and market risks, is pivotal for asset safety because a lower level of these risks tends to be linked with higher liquidity. However, high market liquidity depends on a wider array of factors, including ease and certainty of valuation, low correlation with risky assets, and an active and sizable market, among others. Importantly, different investors place a different emphasis on each of these criteria. For example, investors with long-term liabilities—such as pension funds and insurance companies—place limited emphasis on market liquidity and thus consider less liquid, longer-maturity assets as safe. If their potential payoffs are linked to inflation and no inflation-indexed securities are available, pension funds emphasize the real capital preservation aspect of safe assets. Global reserve managers consider all of these aspects in view of the high share of credit instruments denominated in foreign currencies and their need to maintain ready liquidity. Finally, demand for some noncredit instruments, such as gold, is largely driven by perceptions of its store of value, with less regard to its market risk.

Negative Risk-Free Rates

Yields on fixed rate or zero coupon bonds have no boundaries; in theory they could go infinitely negative. Negative yields are no longer uncommon; in Switzerland and Denmark, 1- to 3-year-maturity government bond yields were negative 25 basis points on average, and most of the Treasury bills in Europe, the United States, the United Kingdom, and Japan are also currently trading near zero or even negative. A negative yield implies a cost to the investor, a payment from the creditor to the debtor. That speaks to the fact that a negative yield essentially reflects a bond that is close to default "free" because the creditor, not the debtor, owes principal. Of course, that negative yield is not truly "risk free" because the debtor still has to pay a coupon that it could default on. Buying a bond with a negative yield is a close substitute for cash because it represents a fee people pay to hold deposits or bonds rather than holding cash. How negative nominal rates could go largely depends on the willingness to pay the costs for holding cash. This is also related to expected returns; if those are low, people are willing to accept a low nominal rate as long as the expectations of capital gains remain positive. Thus, do negative yields matter as long as capital gains can be made in Treasury bonds? To find an answer to this question, one may have to look at equities. The idea of negative rates has not been strange to the equity world. According to CFA Institute research, equity risk premium in the United States has been on average −0.91 percent from 1965 to 2007. The negative premium implies an earnings yield (1/price-earnings ratio) "persistently" below the sovereign yield. Both Japan and the United States experienced a negative equity risk premium that reversed after their financial crises. The average long-term equity risk premium has remained positive, however, between +2 and +1.5 percent, respectively. This has been called the "equity premium puzzle." Researchers Prescott and Mehra found that to reconcile high equity returns, relative "negative" earnings yields had no impact on people investing in stocks, simply because they always expected capital gains. Their research showed, however, that the premium puzzle was not caused by high equity returns themselves, but rather by low risk-free rates and cash holdings. In fixed income, the expectation of capital gains is, for instance, expressed by the shape of the yield curve. Also here a "premium puzzle" is at hand: the long-run average slope of the yield curve—simply measured as 10-year versus bill rates—has always been positive. That premium, known as the "term premium," is a mash of many things, including inflation expectations, volatility, liquidity, and now also longer-term fiscal policy risks. Thus, negative yields may not matter as long as the curve exhibits a positive term premium. And indeed, during the last 15 years, when Japan has experienced near zero bond rates and when its bills have traded negative, not just its term premium was positive (an average of 20 basis points, according to the Bank for International Settlements). Thus, investing in a negative yielding bond has to answer to one of three definitions of "term premium":

1. Expected return of a zero coupon bond minus a short rate
2. A forward rate minus an expected future spot rate
3. Zero coupon yield minus average expected short rates

This all has to do with the expectations hypothesis. That states that the expected return from holding a long bond until maturity is the same as the expected return from rolling over a series of short bonds with a total maturity equal to that of the long bond. That is, the long bond yield is the average of the expected short-term rates. The implication of negative rates is vast, however. The repurchase market for collateral borrowing becomes a business of paying money to lend money. Negative repo rates cause collateral "specialness" that works adversely on market liquidity. Negative deposit rates should discourage people from holding cash. The corollary is that when that cash is held at a safeguarded institution such as a central bank, the monetized assets backing those deposits are viewed as default "free." That continues to present a "convenience yield" on holding cash despite its return being negative. A theory is that to really force cash out, "real balances"—the sum of bonds and cash divided by the price level—should be allowed to increase. French economist Pigou called this the "Pigou effect": consumption increases when the real balance of wealth rises during a period of deflation. Rather than using quantitative easing to fight a liquidity trap, holding money has to be made as unattractive as possible to drive money into bonds or stocks and other assets to spur a wealth effect. Economist Barro objected to such a method because wealth from bonds is negated by taxation of their coupons, better known as the "Ricardian equivalence." Negative nominal rates may spur consumption to a degree or could also drive money into tangible assets such as housing. All of this was an effect of the changing nature of government bonds' role in portfolio diversification.

Zero, Cero, Nought, Null, Noppes, Zilch, Noll, Nolla, μηδέν, sıfır

Zero is universal across languages. The number can mathematically not be divided by itself, nor can other numbers be divided by it. Zero is an even number but neither a positive nor a negative number. Zero is a floor, a boundary from which returns on assets can turn negative or positive in real and nominal terms. Since late 2008, most major central bank rates have been near zero. A central bank policy rate cannot go negative because that would imply a view that the economy should grow at a negative rate. By definition, a central bank policy rate is a barometer of future growth and inflation. The zero boundary is therefore a constraint, a limit in using conventional tools. However, the

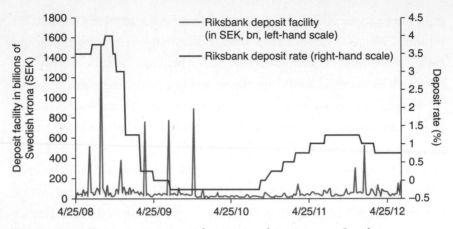

Figure 1.3   First experiment with negative deposit rates, Sweden.
(*Source:* Riksbank, Bloomberg.)

rate on a central bank deposit facility can be negative. Negative rates
have been "experimented" with before. The Swedish Riksbank kept its
deposit rate at −0.25 percent in 2009 and 2010. Unfortunately, that
did not have that much effect on deposit balances at the central bank
(Figure 1.3). In Denmark and Switzerland, deposit rates are negative for
the purpose of maintaining an exchange rate peg. In a press conference
in 2012, European Central Bank (ECB) president Draghi mentioned
three reasons why high levels of cash are desired. High cash is held
because of risk aversion, lack of capital, or lack of funding. Liquidity is
not the problem. The Bank for International Settlements (BIS) has estimated that global central banks have generated approximately $10 tril-
lion in liquidity since the crisis began in 2007. Risk aversion and lack
of capital have kept large sums of cash on the sidelines. Central banks
applied creativity by methods such as credit easing lending schemes and
zero or negative deposit rates to create incentives for deploying cash.
If these are successful, excess liquidity may lead to buildup of capital.
This could especially happen when negative deposit rates or negative
yields on bonds become statutorily unacceptable. The money market

and pension industry were the first to react to negative yields. In 2012, J.P. Morgan and Goldman Sachs stopped inflows to their European money market funds as a result of negative yields. Other money market funds have followed. In general, the rejection of zero or negative rates is putting pressure on the center of financial markets finance. That center is the "risk-free rate" where cash is invested. There is an argument that adding more liquidity to the global financial system by central banks would not achieve the objective of getting cash invested at negative deposit rates out of the system and into the real economy. If true, then all unconventional policies end up in a zero sum game. The investment implications vary. Negative nominal rates may spur consumption to a degree if they reflect risk aversion that has a deflating effect on energy prices. They could also drive money into tangible assets such as real estate, gold, or land. All of this is an effect of a global liquidity trap that is supply and demand driven, similar to a soccer match in which a score of 0 to 0 is an "effortless tie."

A New Steady State

Irving Fisher developed a theory about the relationship between nominal and real (inflation-adjusted) interest rates determined by borrowers and lenders. When borrowers and lenders agree on a nominal interest rate, they have an expectation of inflation but do not know what amount of inflation will be realized over the term of their agreement. Because inflation is assumed to be unknown, the nominal interest rate therefore has the components of an expected real interest rate and an expected inflation rate. This became known as the "Fisher equation," which says that when expectations of real rates and inflation change, nominal market and contractual rates change. St. Louis Federal Reserve president Bullard used the Fisher equation to identify two combinations of nominal rates and inflation known as "steady states," one of which occurs in the absence of any shocks, when nominal rates remain in a "steady state."

When the inflation rate is either very low or negative, nominal short-term rates can move to an "unintended steady state." Figure 1.4 on page 25 from the St. Louis Federal Reserve shows these steady states occurring when the Fisher relationship crosses the line representing the Taylor rule. With the policy rates near zero percent in the developed world and inflation expectations now at around 3 percent (as measured by the 5-year break-even rate on inflation-indexed bonds 5 years forward, a fancy way of looking past current inflation to where markets believe inflation expectations will be in 5 years looking 5 years out), global central bank rates (except for Japan) are currently in between the steady states, as depicted in Figure 1.4. However, unlike what the Fisher equation would describe, even with firmer inflation expectations, it has become less natural for nominal policy rates to adjust higher. When the sovereign debt crisis intensified, the construct of the policy rate became further embedded in the real interest rate demanded on government bonds. Because the debt crisis enforces severe austerity on economies, a risk of deflation remains high and could increase expectations of higher future real borrowing costs. According to the Fisher theory, the borrower and lender would have to agree to a new nominal rate that could be significantly higher. With much higher debt levels and lower growth, higher nominal rates may carry greater risk of insolvency and cause financial instability. The sovereign crisis has created a new steady state in which nominal policy rates have to be low to keep inflation expectations higher so real borrowing costs remain stable. As Figure 1.4 shows, the new steady state would be around a 0 to 1 percent nominal rate with inflation expectations in a range of between 2.5 and 3.5 percent, as opposed to the traditional steady state that prescribes a 3 to 3.5 percent nominal policy rate. In normal times, policy rates would theoretically be adjusted to 3 to 3.5 percent with some degree of synchronized tightening among the world's central banks. In an age of private and public sector debt deleveraging, however, the new steady state aims to prevent deflation rather than inflation. Moreover,

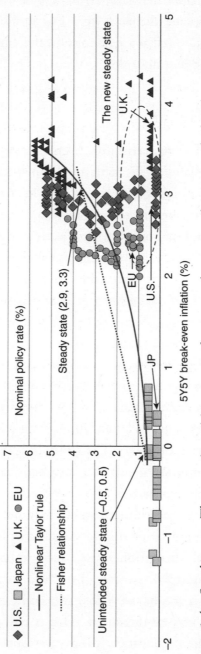

Figure 1.4 Steady states. The sovereign crisis appears to have created a new steady state in which policy rates have to be low to keep inflation expectations higher so real borrowing costs remain stable. Data are from April 2004 to July 2011. (*Source*: St. Louis Federal Reserve, Bloomberg, PIMCO estimates.)

although some central banks may start tightening at some point in the future, the new steady state demands very low nominal policy rates stretched out over time, as well as a reduction in the synchronization of tightening cycles among central banks.

Changes in Diversification

It is known from MPT that maximum diversification is achieved by "buying the market portfolio." Benefits of diversification stem from the basic idea that combining different assets in a single portfolio results in an overall better return-risk profile than holding any of the individual assets. A combination of not perfectly correlated, different assets should produce better expected returns for the same amount of or less risk. In global bond portfolios, diversification became a necessity given paltry returns on core government bonds and higher credit risk in peripheral sovereigns. There was a "migration" visible within sovereign debt markets whereby credit and interest rate risk have seen a distinct change between countries. As can be seen in Figure 1.5 on page 27, a yield convergence reflective of a credit–interest rate risk shift was occurring between countries such as Italy and Spain on the one hand and Mexico on the other. When South Africa was included in the World Government Bond Index (Citigroup index) in 2012, it was another sign of more interest rate convergence between emerging and developed sovereign debt markets.

A portfolio of global government bonds may be a different basket than it was in the past. It revisits the concept of "country betas," defined as the duration attribution from a foreign bond in a home-biased portfolio. By multiplying the country beta (derived from correlation between foreign and home yields) and home-biased duration, a diversification effect can be measured. This is based on yield correlations between different countries, a measurement of the beta that also includes level, slope, and curvature. The return of a foreign bond

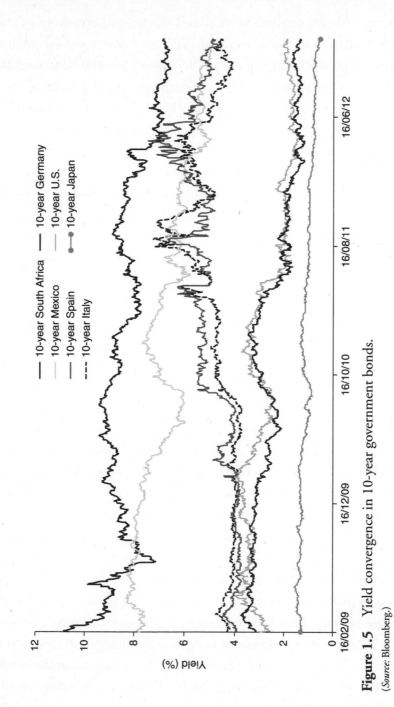

Figure 1.5 Yield convergence in 10-year government bonds.

(*Source:* Bloomberg.)

27

is then partially determined by the level, slope, and curvature of the home base market. By looking at the different betas, a similar picture emerges. Using the United States as the home base, the beta (correlation) has seen the same migration as in the converging yields shown in Figure 1.5. A simple conclusion is that having a bond portfolio solely consisting of German Bunds, Japanese government bonds, U.K. Gilts, and U.S. Treasuries is no longer a well-balanced mix. Since the European debt crisis, all four bond markets have become more strongly correlated with one another than during the financial crisis. This effect has reduced the diversification benefit of mixing U.S. government bonds with foreign government bonds. Diversification became more delicate when government bonds such as those from Italy or Spain are included. Despite their large, domestically active markets, their government bonds were no longer seen as a natural choice as a result of the 2010 to 2012 European sovereign crises. A global bond portfolio has been "forced" to reach out to other markets, such as Mexico, Brazil, South Africa, and Korea, and even several emerging market frontier markets. Investing in these bond markets requires additional liquidity premium compensation on top of credit and country risk, which, despite improved debt profiles, remains prevalent. There are other "natural" choices such as Australia, New Zealand, Canada, Norway, and Sweden. A caveat is that those countries received the luxury of a "bond scarcity," a combination of very low annual government bond issuance and exceptionally large demand in the search for AAA-rated sovereign bond issuers. Because credit risk has increased in some markets, such as Italy and Spain, the correlation between Spanish and Italian bond yields and those of U.S. Treasuries became more negative. That occurred while the correlation of Mexican and some other emerging markets bonds with U.S. Treasury bonds has been more positive. There is also the currency return element in global bonds via hedged and unhedged strategies. It is also known that when risk premiums on high investment grade bonds are narrow, adding a portfolio of global government bonds can at times be an efficient way to potentially reduce portfolio volatility via currency hedging. Nowadays currency returns are very much influenced by central bank activism. And so the choices on how to diversify a global bond portfolio given currency manipulation, sovereign credit deterioration and liquidity, and scarcity concerns are not easy. Before the 2008 financial crisis, the differentiation between emerging and developed market interest rates was made on the basis of "credit risk" versus "interest rate risk." Today that differentiation continues to exist, but a marked "convergence" between the two types of risk has happened within the global bond universe. It has been a remarkable change of perception. Countries that were initially deemed to be interest rate risks are now seen as having higher credit risk. Other factors that influence this perception are credit ratings, liquidity, solvency, and central bank intervention. This caused a demand shift out of certain government bonds by end investors, creating the notion of multiple equilibria. This is a phenomenon in which at different levels of interest rates, there is "equilibrium." Emerging countries such as Mexico have an interest rate level closer to that of Italy because Mexico's rating (BBB+) is the same as Italy's (BBB+), but there is a big difference between the two countries' debt-to-GDP ratio—36 percent for Mexico and 127 percent in 2012 for Italy.

Conclusion: When the Risk-Free Rate Is No Longer Risk Free

Finance theory would say that the risk-free rate is the hurdle rate to discount free cash flows. It also presents an opportunity cost for capital, investment, and spending. When one decides not to take risk, the risk-free rate would be the minimum required rate of return. That depends on the expected risk-free rate of return. Since the financial crisis, the return has been at an "abnormally" low level of 0 percent or negative. The return is also a reflection of what people expect in terms of growth for the overall economy for the foreseeable future. The risk-free rate can be seen as the sum of two kinds of expectations: an expectation of future inflation and an expectation of future real GDP growth. A risk-free rate of 0 percent is a sign of caution and increasing pessimism about the economic health of the global economy. Those feelings and views have pushed down both real growth and inflation expectations. That effect gains momentum in the case of "flight to safety" during a crisis situation. Because this flight to safety affects the risk-free rate, it also affects risk premiums for other securities. Despite the abatement of the 2008 financial crisis, the European debt crisis, and the U.S. debt ceiling and fiscal cliff debacle, flight to safety has increased equity risk premiums. This could have changed expected returns, which consist of the sum of the risk-free rate and an equity risk premium. As a result, the equity risk premium moved closer to 5 percent in 2012, the highest since the 1960s. This has to do with the distortion of the risk-free rate. Based on historical data on equity risk premiums by Ibbotson, at ultra low levels of risk-free rates, the risk premiums represent an "old normal." It creates the perception that, for example, stocks are dramatically undervalued. That may not be fully correct because historical models are using a risk-free rate based on the assumption of growth rates from better times. This would overestimate the value of equities and perhaps other riskier assets such as corporate bonds. To that effect, valuations may appear to be "depressed" (i.e., risk premiums are too narrow). If today's risk-free rate appears to be a rate that is "normalized" to pre-crisis levels, while using risk premiums and growth rates from a crisis period, the estimates of asset values may come out too low. In other words, risk premiums would be too wide. The present-day risk-free rate resembles an "upside-down" world. On the one hand, the rate is distorted by flight to safety and central banks; on the other hand, the risk-free rate is assumed in models to be at an old school value when growth was higher.

There is also a belief that interest rates revert to the mean over time. Using today's risk-free rate and assuming that other inputs than growth rates, cash flows, and premiums will mean revert to pre-crisis levels, a contrarian effect occurs. The exercise churns out a valuation that assumes too quick normalization of current conditions. In fact, valuations are highly dynamic. One would have to use a binomial probability distribution to identify risk premium values over the riskier risk-free rate. For an investor, this is a concern. A changed risk-free rate calls into question the value of other assets and influences decision making. This book attempts to answer that question by looking at the risk-free rate from different angles. Structural forces such as labor market distortions, trade imbalances, population growth, and potential GDP all have an influence on the risks surrounding the risk-free rate. A new set of rules that should allow for more orderly and organized sovereign restructurings is another factor to reckon with. The way risk-free rates should be valued by looking at a complex number of embedded risks is important to understand. This is particularly relevant because the nature of the risk-free rate is to function as a benchmark discount rate to value other assets. This book walks through these elements and provides alternatives investors may consider. It must be said, however, that there are no "alternative risk-free rates as by nature, financial assets all exhibit risks." Milton Friedman once said, "There is no such thing as a free lunch." This book gives investors insight into that statement by presenting a new look at the risk-free universe and what it means when evaluating investments.

Chapter 2

Puzzles

The 2008 financial crisis has left "structural impediments" in the economic landscape. Relationships between inflation, unemployment, productivity, and growth have broken down. As a result, their effect on interest rates has changed, too. This has many academics, policymakers, and investors pondering how this is possible. There are several "puzzles" that seem structural in nature. They play a role in determining the level of risk-free rates. In addition, economic risks continue to linger because imbalances among countries remain large. These economic risks have changed the nature of how major advanced economies' sovereign risks are judged. For investors, it is relevant to understand the nature of economic risks and puzzles. The following subsections address each in detail.

The Phillips Curve Puzzle

A speech by Janet Yellen, vice chair of the Board of Governors of the Federal Reserve System, in April of 2012 titled "The Economic Outlook and Monetary Policy" contained analysis that focused on a "puzzle." The question Yellen posed was, why is it that real gross domestic product (GDP) struggles to advance, yet the unemployment rate has been gradually falling? Five years earlier, in early 2007, Yellen's speech titled "The US Economy in 2007: Prospects and Puzzles" addressed the same problem. Then it was the reverse question: why did the unemployment rate not rise when real GDP growth was moderating? A striking resemblance was the combination of unemployment and inflation. In April 2007, the unemployment rate stood at 4.5 percent, and headline inflation registered 2.7 percent. In April 2012, the unemployment rate was at 8.2 percent, and inflation was at 2.7 percent. Thus, 2007 and 2012 had something in common: a soft landing in 2007 was equivalent to a sluggish recovery in 2012. In both cases, the mystery variable was the unemployment rate, known for its lagging nature. Yellen pointed out that a reason for the change in the relationship between growth and unemployment is the law of economics, or "Okun's law." Yellen argued the law may be broken. In brief, Okun's law describes the relationship between employment and GDP. The main rule of thumb is that for every 1 percent increase in the unemployment rate, a country's GDP will be roughly 2 percent lower than its potential GDP. The Federal Reserve has put emphasis on Okun's law being less applicable because of a structural change in the labor market. There is another economic "law" that also saw a shift. Before Arthur Okun presented his thesis in 1962, William Phillips introduced the concept of the "Phillips curve" in 1958. This is an inverse relationship between unemployment and inflation. There are "short-run" and "long-run" Phillips curves. Phelps, Friedman, and others have argued that the short-run curve signifies a monetary policy decision trade-off between inflation and unemployment. The long-run curve is vertical because, as Friedman and Phelps argued, there is one level of unemployment—the non-accelerating inflation rate of unemployment (NAIRU)—at which inflation is "stable." The NAIRU is the natural rate of unemployment, an equilibrium level from which inflation can accelerate when actual unemployment is below or decelerate when unemployment is above the natural rate. NAIRU has "built-in" inflation. When inflation stays too high and unemployment too low, a wage–price spiral could cause high inflation at different unemployment rates. Too low inflation and too high unemployment lead to the reverse. In Figure 2.1 on page 36, the basic Phillips curves are depicted, where the "old" curve (1995–2007) has a classic downward-sloping shape. The "new" curve (2008–2012) has shifted more to a vertical position. If the Phillips curve theory were applied, a conclusion could be that the unemployment rate would not be too far off NAIRU. There has been a debate that since the 2008 crisis, NAIRU has shifted higher as unemployment stayed stubbornly high. In the Federal Reserve's central tendency forecasts since 2009, the long-run unemployment rate has moved to 6 percent. That said, estimating how high NAIRU is remains quite difficult. If Figure 2.1 is true, it suggests that NAIRU would be closer to 6.5 percent. Key to NAIRU is to what degree the unemployment rate under- or overstates labor market conditions. Variables such as wages, time lag, Conference Board index job perceptions, hard-to-fill–plentiful jobs index, job openings and labor turnover survey (JOLTS), skill mismatch, and the "Beveridge curve" (vacancies versus unemployment rate) are indicators that measure the tightness or looseness of the labor market. The vertical shape of the Phillips curve—if persistent—is an indication of potential difficult future trade-offs the Federal Reserve has to make between inflation and unemployment. That has implications for the fed funds rate and thereby also for short-term interest rates.

A great concern among economists is that "hysteresis"—the fraction of unemployed persons who are out of work longer than 6 months—creates an economy-wide skill mismatch that increases structural unemployment. Another effect of hysteresis is the available pool of labor. When this pool further shrinks as a result of people not being able to find work that fits their skill set, the labor force participation rate can fall, which in turn lowers the unemployment rate.

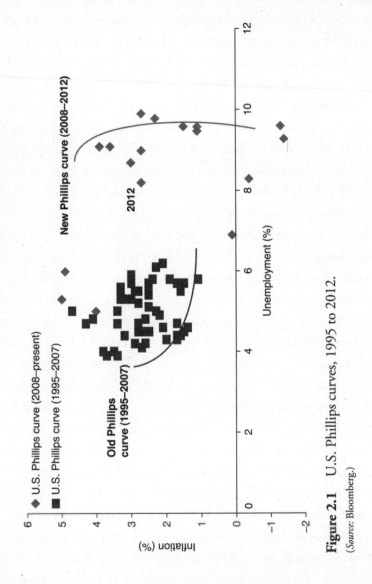

Figure 2.1 U.S. Phillips curves, 1995 to 2012.
(*Source:* Bloomberg.)

A side risk is that when hysteresis festers in the labor market, it entices those who are employed to demand higher wages because they see themselves as being in a stronger bargaining position. If successful, this can lead to "pattern bargaining," a phenomenon that led to a wage–price spiral in the 1970s. The Phillips curve theory based on wage growth would say that as NAIRU is higher, nominal wages are to catch up as inflation is rising. There is a triangle behind inflation driven by "demand inflation" as hysteresis entices wage bargains, "shock-supply inflation" as commodity prices remain elevated, and "inflation inertia" driven by inflation expectations that have an impulse. What may therefore not necessarily be concluded from Figure 2.1 is that the vertical curve shape with a higher NAIRU says that inflation is indeed stable. The Federal Reserve has argued that because the unemployment rate is subject to a very gradual decline, inflation is subject to transitory effects. In part out of fear, the U.S. Phillips curve does end up like that in Japan, flatter at a lower unemployment rate, but mirrored in deflation as displayed in Figure 2.2 on page 38. To prevent that from happening, the Federal Reserve and other central banks have committed themselves to keeping interest rates low for a long time.

Because NAIRU is viewed as time varying, commodity prices are seen as eventually affecting inflation negatively through tighter financial conditions. Moreover, judging wage gains as subdued because productivity has risen ignores the idea that a higher unemployment rate does not diminish the probability of inflation expectations shifting structurally higher. The vertical shape in Figure 2.1 shows that at different unemployment and inflation rates, a "Phillips curve puzzle" is at work. That vertical shape has given monetary policymakers the idea that "reflation," or inducing price levels to recover to their normal trend, is necessary. This can cause momentum in market-based inflation expectations. Thus far, the Federal Reserve has not seen NAIRU as uncomfortably higher. Structural unemployment being a key objective to balance the dual mandate has continued to promote

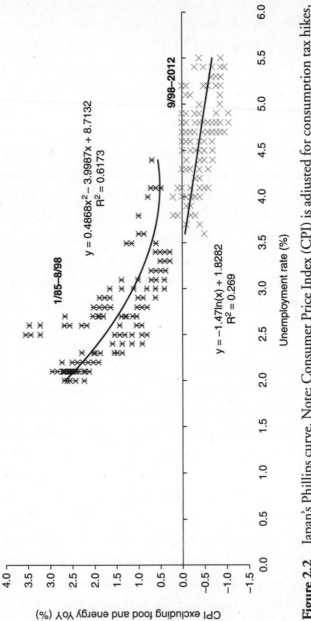

Figure 2.2 Japan's Phillips curve. Note: Consumer Price Index (CPI) is adjusted for consumption tax hikes, year over year % (YoY).

(*Source:* Japan Ministry of Internal Affairs and Communication (MIC) and Credit Suisse.)

a stance toward making risk-free assets riskier (i.e., forcing investors out of the risk spectrum).

The Productivity Puzzle

In his 2002 speech "Productivity," Alan Greenspan discussed the factors that contributed to a wedge between output per hour and economic growth. At that time in 2002, the United States was experiencing high productivity coming off the 1990s driven by labor cost cutting, work processes reorganization, profit margins squeeze, and competitive price pressures. Greenspan recognized a lag process between productivity and GDP growth that was created by "multifactor productivity" caused by technological changes that spurred organizational improvements. To that extent, there was in the early 2000s still a wide "technology gap" in the United States. The gap presents the difference between the productivity of leading-edge capital and the average productivity embodied in the current capital stock. The relevance of the productivity surge was its relation to inflation, which Greenspan judged to be circular because productivity growth can depress labor unit costs and thereby prices. As it were, productivity in later years (2004–2007) fell when real GDP expanded, only to surge after the financial crisis when there was a sharp fall in real GDP. Recent Federal Reserve research (Gratten/Prescott) compared the 1990 to 2003 and 2008 to 2011 periods of above- and below-trend productivity. They found another explanation for the productivity puzzles: "intangible capital." This capital consists of know-how on research and development, compliance, regulatory issues, advertising, branding, and so forth that is expensed rather than capitalized and therefore excluded from GDP. This can distort the picture because when output falls and measured productivity is high, total output includes all unmeasured investment (intangible capital). The actual fall in productivity would then be underestimated. Intangible capital investment, having become a greater part of GDP

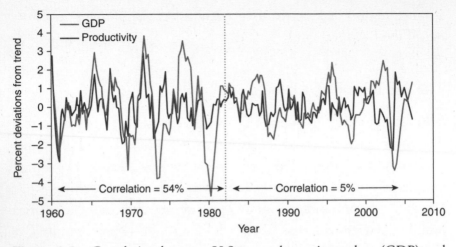

Figure 2.3   Correlation between U.S. gross domestic product (GDP) and productivity.
(*Source:* Federal Reserve.)

but not measured, has changed the correlation between GDP and productivity, from 54 percent during 1960 to 1980 to 5 percent from 1990 to 2011 (Figure 2.3). Productivity in the United States seems to have a less procyclical nature, in part because the fall in the market value of U.S. businesses during 2008 and 2009 of 30 percent was attributable to a sharp fall in intangible capital. Another productivity puzzle resided in the United Kingdom. The Bank of England's Inflation Reports have paid special attention to the phenomenon. U.K. employment has seen decent growth since the 2008 crisis, yet U.K. productivity has fallen and remains 10 percent below the late 2007 peak. The Bank of England addressed several factors contributing to this difference. For instance, statistical flaws, labor hoarding, part-time and self-employment, tighter credit conditions, less lending to dynamic start-ups, and forbearance on loans allow a greater share of less productive firms to operate in the economy. Similar to the case in the United States, the United Kingdom also experienced a large fall of intangible investment that could have pushed down supply capacity.

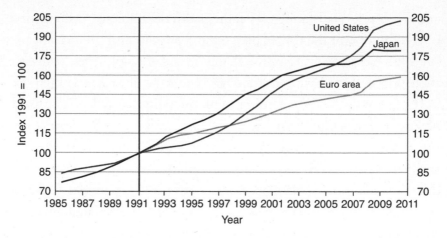

Figure 2.4 Capital-hours ratios for the United States, Japan, and Europe. Gross real capital stock divided by aggregate hours for the whole economy.
(*Sources:* Organisation for Economic Co-operation and Development, Haver Analytics, Citi Research.)

Citigroup economist Nathan Sheets analyzed the evolution of the "capital-hours ratio," gross real capital stock, and aggregate hours worked in the economy. His observation was that particularly the euro area (including the United Kingdom) has been weaker in capital to hours worked, as shown in Figure 2.4. In more detail, it was the fall in hours worked in Europe that has contributed to a lower capital-hours ratio. In other words, there has been less productivity relative to capital expansion in Europe than elsewhere. The productivity puzzle in Japan, on the other hand, has been caused by a change in demand for labor, reflected particularly by demographic changes that led to a higher participation rate of women. The conclusion from productivity puzzles is that the size and scope of the output gaps across the developed world remain in question. Lower productivity suggests a lower level of potential output, which may mean that actual growth is closer to potential, typically linked to a risk of higher inflation.

When viewed in terms of labor unit costs, businesses could face higher growth in labor costs for a period of time. That squeezes margins and forces prices to be raised. That thesis also ties into the "Phillips curve puzzle," where for the United States, the change in unit labor costs since the 2008 crisis has outpaced the change in the unemployment rate even though labor costs have been subdued. The Bank of England noted that unit labor costs have kept rising as productivity has fallen. The Bank of England suggested that payments to pension schemes were a reason. Even though this happened, wage settlements showed a weakening trend. A key question from the productivity puzzle is how labor productivity continues to develop in major advanced economies given the structural nature of unemployment. Nathan Sheets estimated, based on his empirical research, that labor productivity should keep a 1.5 percent pace across major economies. Research by Janet Yellen of the Federal Reserve estimated a long-run level of 2 to 2.5 percent. Productivity being a puzzle, the complexities may mask the true nature of its trend, and labor slack could continue to be underestimated. In the past, large dips in productivity have coincided with higher inflation in the United States and the United Kingdom. The mystery of falling productivity is a risk that can backfire when ultra-loose monetary policies are defended by the argument that the puzzle is ill understood.

Diminishing Returns of Growth

A provocative paper by Robert Gordon titled "Is U.S. Economic Growth Over?" showed that "general purpose technology" in the late 1900s—electricity, combustion, sewerage, and communication—transformed life. This technology caused an explosion in productivity in the twentieth century. It is a source of growth that is lacking today. The key point of Gordon's research is that U.S. productivity has fallen back to the 1972 to 1996 average of 1.3 percent, implying that a "demographic dividend" is in reverse, as retiring baby boomers lower their hours and output per capita. The *Economist's* edition of October 6, 2012, cited this as the "next crisis." Those who retired at age 65 years in 2010 will receive 17 times more than what they will pay in taxes, leaving a hefty bill for future generations. Gordon points to six headwinds—income inequality, debt, demographics, education, environment taxes, and globalization—to future output. Subtracting each of these from the 1987 to 2007 1.8 percent average, real long-run U.S. output could be just 0.2 percent by 2100 (see Figure 2.5 on page 44).

In early 2009, the notion among economists and investors grew that the financial crisis had been so severe that it might have permanently eliminated parts of the total output in major advanced economies. The massive amount of layoffs after the crisis in the financial sector, real estate, automotive, and other related service sectors caused not only a mismatch in labor skills, but also a loss of a generation of existing and future jobs that would no longer be recovered. The financial crisis taught how flawed the financial system was. Thus, greater oversight and regulation were needed to rein in any buildup of excesses. Examples of increased regulation are Dodd-Frank on banks' proprietary risk taking, Basel III on higher capital requirements, and Solvency II requirements on the insurance and pension industry. These regulations meant that the use of capital leverage by financial institutions to boost earnings and return on equity had changed. That also implied that as a result, financial institutions would be less inclined to expand their balance sheets with loans to the private sector, in part as the demand for loans diminished because of the financial crisis's effect on structural unemployment. This change in the structure of large, advanced economies' building on credit creation and services, as well as demographic declines in terms of births and graying of the population, meant that potential GDP had fallen below pre-crisis levels. Policymakers acknowledged this fall in potential GDP by late 2012. Federal Reserve chairman Ben Bernanke and Bank of England governor Mervyn King both said that a robust economic recovery would take much longer than what the past had shown. Potential GDP as the sum of labor productivity and population growth is an important determinant of asset returns. The

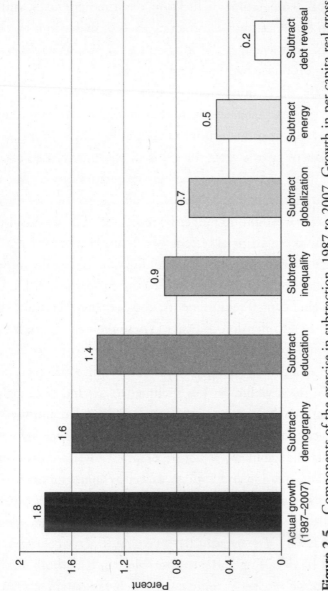

Figure 2.5 Components of the exercise in subtraction, 1987 to 2007. Growth in per capita real gross domestic product to hypothetical future growth in real consumption per capita for the bottom 99 percent.

(*Source:* Robert Gordon, Northwestern University.)

	Average 1987–1996	Average 1997–2006	2007	2008	2009	2010	2011	2012	2013
				Potential GDP					
France	2.1	1.9	1.7	1.7	1.2	1.3	1.4	1.5	1.6
Germany	2.1	1.8	1.5	1.5	1.2	1.1	1.4	1.6	1.5
Italy	1.7	1.4	0.8	0.6	0.2	0.2	0.3	0.3	0.3
Japan	2.5	1.4	0.6	0.6	0.5	0.6	0.6	0.7	0.8
Netherlands	3.0	2.8	1.7	1.7	1.3	1.1	1.1	1.2	1.3
Spain	2.5	3.2	2.8	2.3	1.4	1.3	1.2	1.2	1.2
United Kingdom	2.3	2.9	1.6	1.4	0.9	0.9	0.9	1.1	1.3
United States	3.1	2.9	2.3	2.2	1.8	1.7	1.9	2.0	2.1
Total OECD	2.8	2.6	2.0	1.9	1.5	1.5	1.6	1.7	1.8

Figure 2.6 Potential gross domestic product (GDP) change in major advanced economies.

(*Source:* Organisation for Economic Co-operation and Development [OECD].)

Organisation for Economic Co-operation and Development (OECD) publishes forecasts of potential GDP (Figure 2.6) showing how current and future potential GDPs are lower than long-run averages for major economies.

Other Economic Risks: A Balance of Payments Crisis

Under a fixed exchange rate regime, changes in international reserves can materially affect an exchange rate peg. The central bank that controls reserves sometimes does not have the upper hand. In that context, Paul Krugman analyzed in a 1979 paper what he called a balance of payments crisis. A country pegs its currency through market intervention, and when reserves gradually decline, a sudden currency attack can occur. The attack can be driven by the market's recognition of a central bank's inability to defend the currency peg because its resources (currency reserves) are exhaustible. Krugman argued that when the market knows the central bank has committed part of its reserves to defend the currency peg, a speculative attack can swallow the remaining stock of reserves, leaving a central bank depleted and the peg fully exposed. As Krugman states: "When a central bank is no longer able to defend a fixed parity because of constraints on its actions, there is a 'crisis' in the balance of payments." The balance of payments played a key role in 2011 during the height of the European debt crisis. Specifically, in a monetary union, sharp private capital outflows that well exceed the current account and are insufficiently offset by official intervention can lead to a "sudden stop." When sudden capital flows happen because of nonresidents withdrawing their portfolios en masse, it is a balance of payments crisis when those capital outflows exceed the current and capital accounts.

The European balance of payments crisis fell into the category of "twin deficits hypotheses." When an economy is borrowing from foreigners to finance trade and fiscal deficits while domestic savings remain the same or fall, "sudden" currency depreciation or a rise in domestic interest rates can occur. The fact that European Economic and Monetary Union (EMU) countries borrow in a foreign currency (the euro) that they cannot control has left governments unable to guarantee cash available at all times to creditors. The creditors recognized this inability, and their withdrawal from peripheral bond markets left current account and fiscal deficits further vulnerable. Although there was official intervention from the European Central Bank (ECB) with Long Term Refinance Operations, the Securities Market Program, and Emergency Liquidity Assistance as well as bailout transfers from the European Union and the International Monetary Fund (IMF), private capital flows were only partially offset. This left interest rates in countries such as Spain and Italy well above their pre–2008 crisis average.

Belgian Professor Paul De Grauwe identified this change as the underlying "fragility" of the euro system. There is financial fragility, as the difference in definition between liquidity and solvency narrows during distress times. The "real fragility" reflects the imbalances among countries in terms of competiveness, growth, and twin deficits. The secular kind of risk is "social-political rejection" that through the higher frequency of falling governments and new elections sees more extreme political movement against austerity and increased calls for euro exit. Fragility is connected to asymmetry, what De Grauwe described as the "incomplete monetary union" where one (or two) countries set rules for others and enforce them. As imbalances grow, so does asymmetry when more austerity and reforms are enforced. This brings into doubt a government's ability to maintain payments to its creditors. Creditors withdraw their capital, recognizing the worsening loop between a country's fragility and the forced austerity measures its government has to take. The balance of payments crisis model analyzes interaction between the government and the central bank and how each would behave when a sudden crisis strikes. On the one hand, the central bank allows the stock of private credit to expand. The fixed exchange rate can become floating when reserves fall to zero. On the other hand, the government could borrow from the central bank more directly to finance the deficit. That would increase the central bank's claims on the government and limit its ability to borrow foreign reserves to defend the currency. In the case of the euro zone, there is legal limit on governments and central banks borrowing from and lending to each other. It is to a degree the private capital flows that function as reserves for the euro system, providing financing through domestic fixed income markets. Those private flows caused deposit outflows from peripheral countries in the south to core countries in the north of Europe. It has caused an exhaustion of available capital and reserve resources that has made the EMU more vulnerable to future sudden reversals in capital flows. As a result of the ongoing sovereign crisis, the imbalances between European countries have swelled. The European Central Bank publishes TARGET2 balances. The term stands for "Trans-European Automated Real-Time Gross Settlement System." It is a system in which the national central banks in Europe finance each other's current account. This financing is reported as claims and liabilities to the euro system balance sheet. These claims and liabilities run through the national central banks and their domestic banks. The difference between Germany's claims on the one hand and Spain, Italy, and Greece's liabilities on the other grew very wide, as shown in Figure 2.7 on page 49. This had an adverse effect on interest rates; whereas German interest rates fell sharply, those of Italy, Spain, and several other peripheral countries rose. Perceptions of what were once regarded as risk-free European sovereigns entirely changed.

Economic Risks: Capital Flight

Related to the balance of payments crisis is capital flight. It refers to a rapid flow of money or assets caused by a change in taxation or by fear of capital controls, default, and expropriation. When investors anticipate such measures, the flight of capital lowers the value of assets. That by itself reinforces further capital withdrawal. When debtor countries experience private capital outflows, this erodes net inflows into domestic capital markets. That in turn can increase the cost of debt service. Consequently, this generates concern about the prospects for debt repayment. When one debtor nation faces a likelihood of default, in a currency union, it could increase the expected tax obligations of other countries. This incentivizes their domestic borrowers to place their own funds abroad, thereby increasing the possibility of default on their loans as well. Capital flight arises as a form of contagion. In past emerging markets crises, capital flight has been associated with (hyper) inflation and an anemic state of the banking sector. Combined, these factors typically caused large-scale deposit runs that provoked capital controls and a parallel currency. Carmen Reinhart estimated from parallel currency premiums (difference between parallel and official exchange rates) that when such a premium is high, massive capital flight occurs. Such flight has been a precursor of hyperinflation preceded

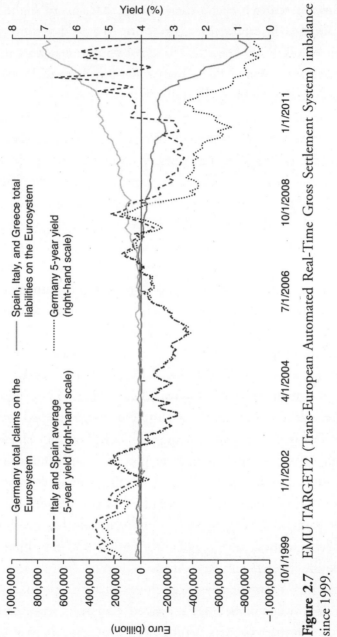

Figure 2.7 EMU TARGET2 (Trans-European Automated Real-Time Gross Settlement System) imbalance since 1999.

(*Source:* Bloomberg, the European Central Bank [ECB].)

by defaults on foreign currency debt and capital market access loss. Federal Reserve research (Schineller) shows that capital flight is also related to social-political fracture, amounting to capital outflows of 5 to 10 percent of GDP on average. The most common factors in flight are countries with twin deficits, high inflation, overvalued exchange rates, and excessive financial liberalization. Capital flight also occurs when the capital account gets restricted, an IMF program requires significant macroeconomic adjustment, or significant political events happen. When capital flight reaches a perceived maximum, it can sharply reverse. Notably, when fiscal and macro adjustments are underway and anticipated to be fruitful, large inflows occur despite interim market volatility. Federal Reserve and Reinhart research shows that when signs of stabilization emerge, repatriation of capital follows swiftly. However, capital inflows remained fragile in, for example, the case of the 1994 Mexican peso crisis, which saw capital flight recurring because of political events. Capital flight remains a key risk to any country. Overindebtedness, distrust in the political system, and social tensions can quickly turn capital away. Table 2.1 shows that parallel market premiums fall and capital flight abates when hyperinflation ends.

A paper presented at the August 2012 Jackson Hole Economic Symposium addressed an important topic of focus for policymakers: *contagion*. The paper, titled "The Big C," identified four channels of contagion. These are trade links, leveraged banking systems, international investors' portfolios, and "wake-up calls" (investors' reappraisal of a country's fundamentals). For example, when a financial shock in one country impairs funding and liquidity in another or when the terms of debt restructuring reveal information on how other countries could be treated similarly, investor capital flight can unfold. The paper's quantitative analysis concludes that Europe in particular is subject to contagion because increased economic integration has removed cross-border barriers. Unique to Europe are the risk of bank runs because of large intramarket exposures and the current liability

Table 2.1   Emerging Markets Capital Flight

	Average Parallel Market Premium* (%)		
	$t-3$	t	$t+3$
Argentina (1989–1990)	66.7	67.7	10.9
Bolivia (1984–1985)	54.0	119.1	7.3
Brazil (1989–1990)	111.5	102.3	18.1
Peru (1990)	278.8	32.7	6.4
Ukraine (1991–1994)	NA	NA	11.1
	Cumulative Capital Flight† (millions of dollars)		
	From $t-3$ to t	During t	From t to $t+3$
Argentina (1989–1990)	8,662	7,938	–27,434
Bolivia (1984–1985)	73	190	–70
Brazil (1989–1990)	38,757	–8,932	–30,476
Peru (1990)	2,310	–669	–11,318

N/A, not available; *t*, the hyperinflation years (in parentheses).
*The parallel market premium is defined as 100 * (ep - e)/e, where ep is the parallel market exchange rate and e is the official exchange rate. For Argentina, Brazil, and Peru, the estimates of capital flight end in 1992 (i.e., $t+2$).
†A positive entry indicates capital flight (an outflow); a negative entry indicates capital repatriation (an inflow).
(*Sources:* World Currency Yearbook (various issues) and Reinhart and Savastano (2002), Carmen Reinhart, "Capital Flows to Latin America: Is There Evidence of Contagion Effects?" [Washington, DC: Institute for International Economics, 1996], 151–171.)

sharing structure between the ECB and the stability mechanisms, the European Stability Mechanism and European Financial Stability Fund. When one or more countries have to access resources from those mechanisms, it increases contingent liabilities for other countries that back the resources with capital or guarantees. That could lead to rating agency actions. A credit rating change for one country has been shown to affect spreads for other countries. A key factor is that institutional minimum ratings could cause portfolio shifts that have to switch downgraded securities for others. If that process continues, it causes a circular motion of causation. That is, ratings affect bond spreads, which worsen sovereign credit ratings, and so on. Contagion can be defined as "fundamentals based" when a country is infected via trade finance. There is also "true contagion" when a common shock suddenly changes perceptions. Carmen Reinhart's research shows that perception change tends to be associated with herding behavior by investors that have large globally diversified portfolio assets. These assets, being hedged cross-market, exhibit high asset returns correlations and co-movement of assets from infected countries. That could cause contagion via hedges that need to be unwound. The Jackson Hole study showed that this kind of correlation is very high for the euro area; specifically portfolio investments, flows, and credit ratings exhibit statistical significance for the four channels of contagion. Considering globalization and significant improvements in technology and information transfer, contagion risks have increased since the 1990s. This has increased the frequency of crises since the 1980s. In Reinhart's work titled "Two Hundred Years of Contagion," she found evidence of repetitive contagion effects across major economies as a result of financial liberalization and high capital mobility.

Economic Risks: Politics of Policy and Policy Uncertainty

In a 2012 *Financial Times* op-ed titled "How Romney Could End Quantitative Easing," Bruce Bartlett made the argument that a change within the Federal Reserve may happen in the future. This would be through existing members' expiring terms. Bartlett reasoned that whoever would be the next chairman of the Federal Reserve in 2014 has to be a board member. Because a candidate with different ideas from the Federal Open Market Committee's (FOMC's) status quo could be in the race for future chairperson, the balance between the "hawks" and the "doves" within the FOMC may change. Whether this will happen or not, it poses an economic risk given how deep the Federal Reserve policy has dug into unconventional territory. In political economics, the changing balance of power within the Federal Reserve could be analyzed along the concept of "rent seeking." An aspect of rent-seeking behavior is to spend public resources to gain an increased share of existing wealth rather than to create new wealth. A critique has been that quantitative easing (QE) is merely a wealth transfer from savers to wealthy risk takers through bad inflation (food and gas prices). Open critics of Federal Reserve policy such as Plosser and Fisher say such wealth transfer has limited effectiveness on the economy and hampers proper market functioning. This has been viewed as nebulous by Bernanke and other members of the FOMC. And as such, a political vicious circle may develop. People perceive that the market mechanism does not function in a way compatible with social and economic goals. A political consensus to temper the Fed's market intervention through ongoing bond purchases could emerge. The political resistance to Fed policy has a risk of putting the Fed chairman in a lame duck position. That creates uncertainty and division about the future of QE at a time when more policy action may still be needed. The political vicious circle could create a delicate balance between Fed members who are considered to be hawkish (in favor of tighter policy) and those who are dovish. Many times this balance is analyzed along the dove–hawk scale, as seen in Figure 2.8 on page 54. This scale as of the end of 2012 shows an estimate of Fed members considered dovish or hawkish, measured by their published opinions on the outlook for Fed policy. The term "change of chairman" is an event of policy change. This can have implications for short-term interest rates in the future.

The Bank of England publishes on its website the history of voting patterns of the Monetary Policy Council (MPC). The history of decision or no decision is a measure of the trend in division among MPC members. The division has grown in part because of rates that needed to be kept near zero and in part because QE decisions were put off. The division had an effect on 10-year U.K. government bond yields, which trailed slowly lower over time. Lower interest rates against the background of

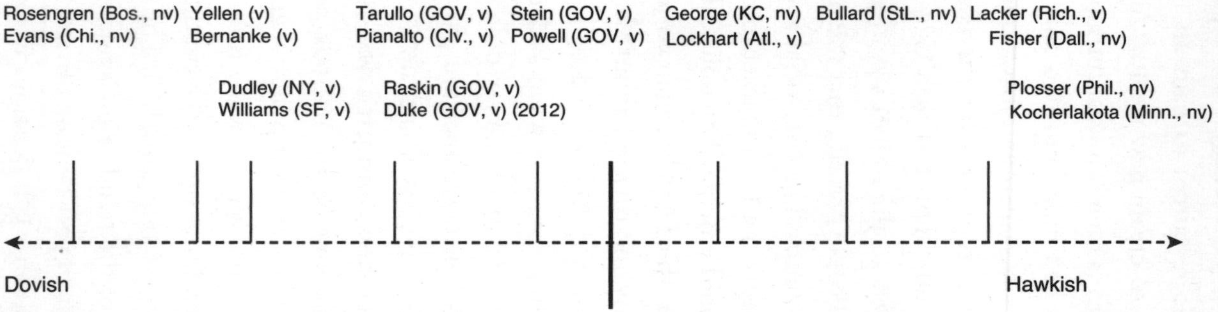

Rosengren (Bos., nv)   Yellen (v)   Tarullo (GOV, v)   Stein (GOV, v)   George (KC, nv)   Bullard (StL., nv)   Lacker (Rich., v)
Evans (Chi., nv)   Bernanke (v)   Pianalto (Clv., v) Powell (GOV, v)   Lockhart (Atl., v)   Fisher (Dall., nv)

                        Dudley (NY, v)   Raskin (GOV, v)   Plosser (Phil., nv)
                        Williams (SF, v) Duke (GOV, v) (2012)   Kocherlakota (Minn., nv)

Dovish   Hawkish

Figure 2.8 Federal Reserve dove–hawk scale, 2012. GOV, board of governors; v, voting member; nv, non-voting member.
(*Source:* J.P. Morgan.)

54

uncertainty surrounding Bank of England policy is another example of risks that can overhang an economy. In Japan, a change of Bank of Japan's chairman in 2013 saw political pressure to engage in more unconventional policy.

In Europe, political choices to implement the required amount of austerity became a vicious circle as well. When a country announced fiscal measures to counter a declining economy, markets would react negatively because the measures were seen as further contributing to economic decline. Consequently, a weaker economy would suffer worsening debt and deficit projections that led to expectations of ratings downgrades, which caused bond yields to rise. Higher yields provoked more austerity, which fueled expectations of a greater slide in economies, further pressuring yields. Part of this circle was neutralized by the prospect of an unlimited ECB intervention. The social-political aspects such as mass demonstrations against austerity have not been stabilized by the ECB. These demonstrations reduce economic activity and thereby growth, and are likely to require more austerity to maintain deficit targets. In other words, the European political vicious circle could remain in effect for some time. The policy uncertainty remains very high in Europe and in the United States as well, as shown by the "policy uncertainty index" in Figure 2.9 on page 56. These indices were developed by Scott Baker, Nick Bloom, and Steven Davis. The index measures three types of underlying components: (1) newspaper coverage of policy-related economic uncertainty, (2) the number of federal tax code provisions set to expire in future years, and (3) disagreement among economic forecasters as a proxy for uncertainty. Although there is subjectivity in these indices, historically they track interest rates closely. As also shown in Figure 2.9, when uncertainty spiked, interest rates would be cut or fall. Now that policy rates are at zero, the policy uncertainty has risen further to new highs. The market anticipation of political changes is becoming a greater factor as those changes tie into growth forecasts and thereby central bank action.

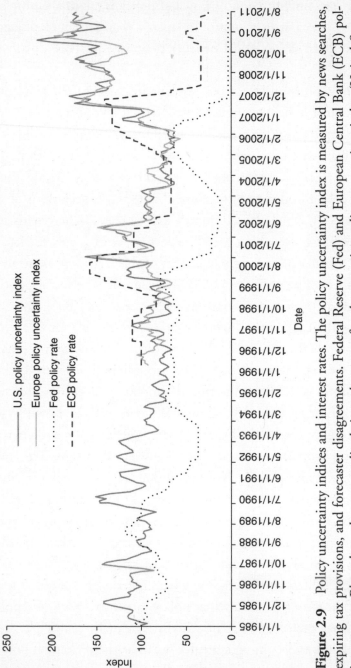

Figure 2.9 Policy uncertainty indices and interest rates. The policy uncertainty index is measured by news searches, expiring tax provisions, and forecaster disagreements. Federal Reserve (Fed) and European Central Bank (ECB) policy rates are Bloomberg data, normalized since the start of each respective policy uncertainty index (United States, January 1, 1985 = 100; Europe, September 1, 1996 =100).

(*Source:* Bloomberg, Stanford.)

Economic Risks: Underestimated Fiscal Multipliers

In the 2012 IMF World Economic Outlook, some attention was paid to "fiscal multipliers." The IMF's key finding was that the fiscal multiplier for advanced economies was around 0.5 pre-crisis but has now shifted higher, toward 1, as a result of forecast errors. Daniel Gros of the Centre for European Policy Studies estimated that the impact of higher fiscal multipliers on output was substantial for the European peripheral countries. The IMF concluded similarly: higher fiscal multipliers are one of the reasons why potential output in the developed world has fallen. What is the investment relevance of this "look-back research"? Higher fiscal multipliers had an impact on potential GDP, acknowledged by the Federal Reserve and the Bank of England. Coming from a lower potential GDP base in order to reach "old normal" nominal GDP, inflation may have to be higher than the pre-crisis average of 2 percent. Table 2.2 shows that 5-year, 5-years-forward rates can be used as a proxy for future return of nominal GDP. The 5-year, 5-years-forward rates were about 1 to 1.5 percent lower than long-run nominal GDP. Nominal GDP is here taken as the sum of the OECD estimate of 2013 potential GDP and the central bank's inflation target. The higher fiscal

Table 2.2 Five-Year, 5-Years-Forward Rates Versus Potential Gross Domestic Product

5-Year, 5-Years-Forward	Level (%)	nGDP*	pGDP*	5-Year, 5-Years-Forward vs. pGDP (%)
U.S.	2.99	4.0	3.9	−0.91
Europe	2.56	2.7	3.4	−0.84
U.K.	3.05	3.9	3.0	0.05
Japan	1.37	−0.4	2.8	−1.43

nGDP, 10-year trailing average gross domestic product (GDP); pGDP, Organisation for Economic Co-operation and Development (OECD) potential GDP for 2013 plus central bank inflation target. *Japan data include a new inflation target.
(*Source:* Bloomberg, OECD as of January 2013.)

multipliers and lower potential GDP suggest that inflation targeting may have to be accomplished by a stated nominal GDP target. At the end of 2012, there was a rapid evolution in global central banking. The Federal Reserve introduced employment and inflation thresholds, the Bank of England investigated the benefits of a potential policy on nominal GDP, and the Bank of Japan adopted a medium-term inflation target. If fiscal multipliers are indeed higher, then higher nominal GDP growth could be induced by higher inflation. Table 2.2 shows in a simple way that at the start of 2013, forward rates in the United States, Germany, and Japan were about 1 percent below nominal GDP measured by potential GDP and the inflation target. With the shift in global central banking toward generating growth by allowing perhaps higher than pre-crisis average inflation, also here the comparison shows that "risk-free" rates are different from what the levels of potential GDP suggest.

Conclusion: Convergence

The IMF 2012 World Economic Outlook showed that interest rate– growth differentials were positive (rates > growth) for many developing markets and negative (rates < growth) for advanced markets. There is a trend toward narrowing the gap, however, as growth rates in emerging markets are falling relative to those in developed markets. In terms of the ratio of debt to GDP, there are signs of convergence, too. The IMF report shows that debt-to-GDP ratio differences between the emerging and the developed world are projected to decline in the coming years. In addition, the maturity of debt for major developed markets has lengthened by 1 year since 2008 to about an average of 8 years, according to the IMF. This is matching more closely the average maturity of emerging markets' external debt. All of these are signs of continuous convergence between developed and emerging markets in terms of growth, credit ratings, and interest rates. Given the nature of fiscal adjustment in developed markets, however, the growth forecast gap (about 1 percent) with the OECD potential GDP may be filled only by higher inflation. That is also a convergence that could bring real interest rate differences between developed and emerging markets closer over time. The conclusion is that interest rate and growth convergence between developed and emerging markets is well under way. On the monetary policy front, large buying programs in developed markets drove real interest rates negative. Investor flows sought out higher real yield opportunities in emerging markets. Their central banks responded to these large capital inflows with taxes, currency intervention, and other capital controls. It has been a sequence over the past few years that may continue until there is a complete convergence in real interest rates between developed and emerging markets.

Chapter 3

A Way of Life

The Hippocratic Oath says do harm and bear the consequences. A "no harm fiscal policy" in the short term can question long-term sustainability. This type of do no harm policy is intimately linked to a country's reputation for past and perhaps future defaults. It falls under the definition of "debt intolerance." It is a threshold at which a country's gross debt level is perceived to be no longer safe. The most often watched metric is a country's ratio of debt to gross domestic product (GDP). Whereas the ratio is dynamic, GDP can expand or contract the amount of debt outstanding (through government spending or cuts). Debt can also affect economic growth. It is a number that has become a greater focus over the past years. Most major developed economies have experienced a sharp rise in the debt-to-GDP ratio. International Monetary Fund (IMF) projections show it could rise even further. This has led to questions about the sustainability of debt as well as the creditworthiness of many countries. Beyond a certain point a nonlinear expansion of debt to GDP could occur. IMF economist Delacci has estimated that when debt to GDP remains persistently above 80 percent and the deficit as a percentage of GDP increases by 1 percent, it adds an incremental risk premium to government bond yields. When a "tipping point" is reached, the market's tolerance for debt lowers. This may coincide with a "sudden stop" in which foreign capital withdrawals cannot be offset by domestic capital. This causes a shift in interest rates to a new plateau, a level where debt becomes uncontrollable. Such a scenario can occur when the realization kicks in that a country has high debt intolerance because the weakness of its fiscal structures and financial systems is fully exposed. Carmen Reinhart demonstrated that in such a case, a country often defaults. Reinhart called this "a way of life." The serial defaults of governments are often caused by financial disruption, rogue tax systems, a high degree of tax evasion, and capital flight. It has been empirically proven that when such factors frequently occur, the risk of serial defaulting remains high and cannot be extinguished by a single stroke of financial engineering. On that basis, there is a loose division of "clubs" of countries. There are countries that have unlimited capital market access and those that have only sporadic access. According to the IMF 2012 Fiscal Monitor and World Economic Outlook, the average debt-to-GDP ratios of major advanced economies will reach close to 120 percent by 2017, with countries such as the United States close to 112.5 percent. Given these debt dynamics, the amount of funds available in the form of savings or capital is not sufficient to square off the number of indebted public and private borrowers across major developed economies.

Government budget deficits and debt have an impact on long-run growth because of "crowding out" the amount of private domestic and foreign savings available to support private investment. When a government issues debt to domestic households, businesses, and banks, it diminishes the amount of private savings available to finance investment. To get a balance between savings and investment, higher real interest rates are required. The circular moment occurs when interest rates rise because the perception of debt has changed. Such higher interest rates may attract some savings but are likely to discourage businesses from investing. As domestic interest rates increase above interest rates elsewhere in the world, foreigners are likely to channel more of their savings into the high-debt-burden country. The inflow of foreign funds can cause an excessive appreciation of the highly indebted nation's currency. A currency appreciation creates a competitive disadvantage for domestic companies. Even if the inflow of foreign funds were to completely offset the domestic interest rate rise, the foreign savings must eventually be repaid with interest. Although economic growth might rise, consumption will be lessened by the amount that must be repaid to the rest of the world. Given the complexities of the global economy, such a textbook-type rebalancing might not work so smoothly. With advanced economies around the globe competing for domestic and foreign savings to finance their public debts, financial inflows are likely to require substantially higher interest rate differentials. Smaller financial inflows at high interest rates result in less domestic investment. Likewise, they are likely to initiate bigger exchange rate movements. The high public debt burdens could also complicate central banks' efforts to reduce their large balance sheets. High interest rates raise the costs of funding public debt. Their impact on government debt burdens can become profound if crowding out simultaneously slows economic growth. Under such circumstances, governments might exert pressures on central banks to keep monetary policy relatively easy. Inflation may rise as a result. The beneficial impact of higher inflation on the budget, however, would be only transient because financial markets would quickly demand higher interest rates to compensate for higher inflation. Nominal interest rates would eventually rise further. These are all dynamics of an environment after a financial crisis.

To understand these dynamics, two examples of countries dealing with unsustainable debt loads are analyzed. The first example is the United States. The United States belongs to Reinhart's definition of a club of privilege. It has the reserve currency; an independent central bank that has so far been "willing" to create large amounts of excess reserves; and large, deep, and liquid capital markets. The Congressional Budget Office (CBO) 2012 long-term budget outlook paints a bleak picture, however. Under the CBO's "alternative fiscal scenario," non-interest spending rises to 23 percent of GDP by 2037, while revenues remain behind at 19 percent. Factors such as prevention of declining Medicare payment rates, not stemming growth in Medicare costs, and extension of income tax cuts to 2022 are the CBO's underlying assumptions. Figure 3.1 shows that when the debt-to-GDP ratio balloons, the national debt could become a "marginal mall."

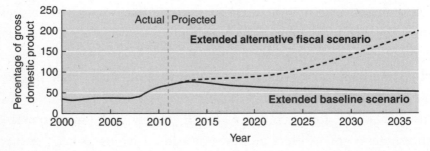

Figure 3.1   Federal Reserve debt held by the public under the CBO's long-term budget scenarios: Congressional Budget Office (CBO) projection. Note: The extended baseline scenario generally adheres closely to current law, following the CBO's 10-year baseline projections through 2022 and then extending the baseline concept for the rest of the long-term project period. The extended alternative fiscal scenario incorporates the assumptions that certain policies that have been in place for a number of years will be continued and that some provisions of the law that might be difficult to sustain for a long period will be modified. Debt does not reflect the economic effects of the policies underlying the two scenarios.
(*Source:* CBO 2012 annual outlook.)

These kinds of malls have high risk of ending in a death spiral when the anchor tenants leave, forcing a default that destroys the crowding in of capital by other tenants. An infinitely rising federal debt crowds out private capital formation and reduces productivity growth. And if it is financed by borrowing from abroad, a growing share of future income would be devoted to interest payments on foreign-held federal debt. When foreign creditors lose faith in the U.S. government's ability to service its debt, they may have a change of heart. Looking at Figure 3.1 more closely, the debt trajectory spirals around 2020 to 2025, and that may be the point where the United States could face a sudden stop in foreign creditor financing.

In a brief analysis around the time of the U.S. fiscal deadline in late 2012, J.P. Morgan's economist Feroli called it the "10-year mirage." The outcome of the fiscal cliff would not really matter because any measures taken did little to address the longer-term fiscal sustainability issues the United States would be facing. Figure 3.2 is a revised version of the CBO's alternative scenario projection. Under a continuation of

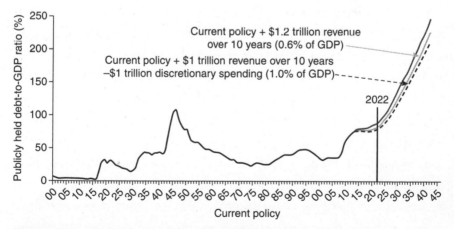

Figure 3.2 Congressional Budget Office (CBO) debt-to-gross domestic product (GDP) projection under current tax and spending policies. (*Sources:* CBO, J.P. Morgan as of 2012.)

tax and spending policies, the debt-to-GDP ratio is projected to reach 247 percent in 30 years. Under the assumption that increases in revenue as a share of GDP would persist after 2022 and including savings from reduced federal debt service payments, the debt-to-GDP was still projected to hit 226 percent of GDP in 30 years. A more fierce way of addressing the problem could have been a trillion dollars in higher revenue coupled with a trillion-dollar reduction in discretionary spending.

Unfortunately, as Feroli showed, the revenue increase and spending reduction as a share of GDP projected forward would still amount to a debt-to-GDP ratio at the end of the 30-year period of an estimated 213 percent. There will be demographic challenges that could further pressure the long-term outlook for the debt-to-GDP ratio around 2025. Estimates by the CBO are that aging of the population accounts for about two-thirds of the increase in social security and federal healthcare spending. The remaining third would come from medical costs.

Figures 3.1 and 3.2 show that indeed, in 10 to 15 years, if there is no meaningful measure taken to bring down the debt, the sudden stop of Treasury debt financing may happen. What can play a key role during a sudden stop is how a country ranks in investors' minds in terms of growth of the external debt-to-GDP ratio. Reinhart's research shows that by using investor surveys, it appears that debt intolerance may happen at even *lower* debt-to-GDP thresholds. Based on a data set of emerging and developed markets countries' debt history, an external debt-to-GDP ratio of 35 to 40 percent is a level where debt intolerance causes a graduation of club membership to less creditworthy sovereign issuers. This graduation is typically accompanied by an adverse credit event such as a default or debt restructuring. Lower interest rates do not necessarily help, even when they are kept low by central banks. New York Federal Reserve and Bank for International Settlements research have shown that the Federal Reserve's bond purchase programs not only lowered long-term interest rates, but also reduced the average maturity of Treasury debt that investors had to otherwise absorb by about

2 years. In other words, the Federal Reserve's purchases of Treasuries took 2 years of duration risk out of the hands of market participants. During this time, the average duration of Treasury debt also lengthened by 2 to 3 years as interest rates fell to record lows. The U.S. Treasury debt held externally is around 32 percent of the total outstanding Treasury debt as of 2012, according to data by the U.S. Treasury. This percentage is near Reinhart's empirically proven threshold of debt intolerance. Because the effectiveness of unconventional Federal Reserve policy was questioned during 2012, a "do no harm fiscal policy" via tax cut extensions may ultimately imply the risk that the CBO's "alternative fiscal scenario" could eventually materialize. One has to understand that obviously other factors, such as innovation and reform of the labor market, can generate higher GDP growth. In the absence of these factors, down the road, the United States may face a situation in which the government would be forced to reduce its debt.

In a *Wall Street Journal* article from November 2012, Chris Cox and Bill Archer argued that the U.S. government debt of $16 trillion outstanding is far larger than it seems. It is a frightening picture of runaway entitlement spending that has gone out of control. With no meaningful reforms having been made, the unfunded pension and healthcare liabilities of the U.S. government have swollen drastically. The main reason why this is not known to the public is lack of transparent financial statements by the government. According to Cox and Archer, the actual liabilities of the federal government, which include social security, Medicare, and federal employees' future retirement benefits, exceed $86.8 trillion, or 550 percent of the U.S. GDP. By the end of 2011, the annual accrued expense of Medicare and social security was close to $7 trillion. The reported budget deficit for 2012 was about $1.1 trillion, or 6.7 percent of GDP, just less than one fifth of the unfunded liabilities. Cox and Archer found in the annual Medicare Trustees' report that there are separate actuarial estimates of the unfunded liability for Medicare Part A (the hospital portion), Part B (medical insurance), and

Part D (prescription drug coverage). The trustees' report of April 2012 shows that the net present value (NPV) of the unfunded liability of Medicare was $42.8 trillion. The comparable balance sheet liability for social security is $20.5 trillion. Such large unfunded liabilities would eclipse world capital markets if the amounts had to be borrowed from foreign creditors. In reality, the Medicare and social security trust funds use 100 percent of payroll taxes to fund themselves, and thus far, this has not resulted in extra borrowing by the U.S. Treasury. Because the payroll taxes are collected and spent in the same year, there is a portion of nonmarketable U.S. Treasury debt that the trust funds currently hold. As Cox and Archer point out, when the baby boomers' benefits that were promised to them overtake the payroll taxes of today's younger generation, at some point the U.S. government will have to swap Medicare and social security trust funds' nonmarketable Treasury debt for marketable Treasury debt. The U.S. Treasury then will have to go out and sell that debt on top of what it already has to borrow from investors. Thus, that moment will be a "tipping point" when the perception of safety of U.S. government debt changes. This is when the realization sets in that indeed there is a marginal mall where tenants rapidly leave. Those tenants could be China and Japan, which combined hold $2.5 trillion of the U.S. Treasury debt in 2012, according to Bloomberg data. Cox and Archer point out further that the accrued expenses of Medicare and social security at about $7 trillion represent the annual growth rate of the government's unfunded liability. Even in the best-case scenario, the U.S. government could not collect enough taxes from individuals and U.S. corporations to cover that accrued expense. Only by containing these spending commitments would U.S. debt get on a sustainable track, and for that, difficult political choices have to be made. The U.S. fiscal cliff debate in 2012 and the debt ceiling debacle of 2011 are minor examples of what is to be expected in the future as the growth of unfunded liabilities has to be dealt with in a more forceful manner.

A different example is Spain. Its past sins show that the country has been a serial defaulter—at least 13 times between 1500 and 1900, according to Reinhart's empirical data. Spain has been a prime example of debt intolerance. The weakness of its financial system became exposed during the summer of 2012, when the IMF and the independent Wyman-Berger consultants held a stress test on Spanish bank assets. Even though the tests showed that the amount of capital Spanish banks needed against their loan books was low (60 billion euros), the European Union had given Spanish loans up to 100 billion euros through the European Stability Mechanism (ESM). The question remained how much of that loan would be added to Spain's national debt, to what extent creditors would be subordinated because of the ESM's preferred creditor status, and how rating agencies would respond. Since the European Summit in June 2012, Spanish bond yields rapidly moved to 7.8 percent as markets discounted the possibility that Spain could be downgraded to junk status. Despite the European Central Bank's open market transactions program, which did lower Spanish interest rates, in the months following, they remained at least 3 to 4 percent above German interest rates. Spain's low level of debt to GDP (66 percent) showed it can become a prerequisite of expectations of future default. Such default weakens institutions that hold the debt, and that can cause more defaults.

Reinhart and Rogoff Revisited

Markets like acronyms. Some have used "the three Rs." They can stand for recession, repression, and risk or rating, rollover, and restructuring. A way out of a debt crisis is recapitalization, rehabilitation, restructuring, and recovery. Whichever way it is said, the three or four Rs have one thing in common: public and private sector deleveraging. This is a topic that continues to receive lots of attention by the media, investors, and academics. The underlying cliché says that solving a debt crisis with liquidity and more debt leads to a further crisis. The leap to the next debt crisis depends on the speed of debt deleveraging. In 2012, McKinsey released a report showing that the United States led the pack of countries where deleveraging in the private sector was well underway, with a reduction of private debt to GDP of about 16 percent since 2008. Deleveraging by reducing total debt (public and private) to GDP can be achieved in five ways. Reinhart has set several criteria for this: (1) more economic growth, (2) substantive fiscal adjustment or austerity plans, (3) explicit default or restructuring of private or public debt, (4) a surprise burst in inflation, and (5) a steady dose of financial repression. These five points connect to the most important conclusion of Reinhart and Rogoff's empirical evidence: the strong relationship between default and inflation. There is a distinction made in the definition of default: it can be either external (debt in foreign currency) or domestic (debt in local currency). In a separate paper, "The Forgotten History of Domestic Debt," Reinhart and Rogoff find that the linkage between default and inflation is especially strong through the domestic debt channel. In most cases of hyper- or high inflation, domestic debt as a percentage of GDP was higher than external debt. These episodes typically saw a fall in output of 8 percent on average in the 3 prior years, which then is followed by significantly higher inflation in the 3 years after the default (Figure 3.3 on page 71). The process of output decline phased into inflation is accompanied by "expropriation" of domestic savers, the concept of financial repression. Reinhart has also shown that there is linkage to episodes of high inflation that occurs when "liquidations years" (the period of time when real yields stay persistently negative) fall together with debt reduction years (the period of time when deleveraging takes place).

To avoid spikes in interest rates, governments tend to "promote" government debt through their banking systems by regulation. Regulation makes the banks actually more vulnerable because they are incentivized to buy government debt. That can be the start of a sovereign

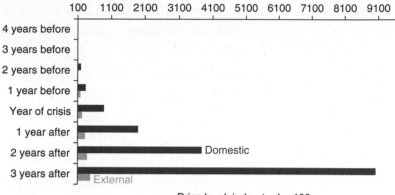

Figure 3.3 Inflation before and after sovereign default.

(*Source:* Reinhart and Rogoff, "The Forgotten History of Domestic Debt," 2008.)

debt crisis down the road. Debt promotion through banks causes variety in crises because when banks suffer loan losses from the private sector, there are typically widespread defaults that follow. This is often accompanied by currency debasement or devaluation. These are factors for inflation, next to high base money as a percentage of GDP. And so, with Greece being the first modern country to have defaulted in a major way, is the stage set for further sovereign defaults crises? And if so, will higher inflation be a certain outcome? For one thing, the global stages of deleveraging vary in speed and nature. In most major economies, the output gap (difference between actual and potential GDP) is negative, but inflation has been modestly on the rise since 2009. The United States, the United Kingdom, Germany, and Japan had a positive real GDP, mainly because of higher inflation as a result of quantitative easing policies. In Europe, Greece has had since late 2008 a cumulative output decline of more than 8.5 percent, and Portugal has had about −3 percent real GDP growth since 2010. Other countries such as Italy and Spain are a year behind and have had an output gap of 1 percent since 2011. So in Reinhart and Rogoff's definition, when Portugal sees closer to

−8 percent real GDP, it probably has to restructure its debt. If Italy and Spain catch up, they will also fall into the category of candidates that are likely to default.

Ray Dalio from Bridgewater Associates added some additional variation by dissecting stages of deleveraging. He sees three types of deleveraging: (1) ugly deflationary deleveraging, (2) beautiful deleveraging, and (3) ugly inflationary deleveraging. Central in these cases is the degree of debt monetization by central banks and governments as the balance between monetization and debt reduction begets choices. In Table 3.1, Dalio shows how "beautiful" deleveraging cases in modern, developed economies took place. It is clear in these examples that the length of deleveraging differs greatly, from as short as 2 to 3 years to as long as multiple decades, such as in Japan. The duration of deleveraging can be reduced in the event of very aggressive monetary policy purchasing government debt. This is called "reflation." It is a monetary policy strategy in which signals to financial markets are used to influence growth via higher inflation expectations (implied from Treasury Inflation-Protected Securities) and higher value of financial assets such as stocks and bonds. The idea is that reflation spills over to the real economy and would boost spending and infrastructure

Table 3.1   "Beautiful" Deleveraging

Monetary policy results during debt deleveraging periods	U.S. 1933–1937	U.K. 1947–1969	U.S. 2009–2012
GDP - 10-year yield	6.3%	1.6%	0.3%
Average GDP	9.2%	6.8%	3.5%
GDP deflator	2.0%	3.9%	1.4%
Real GDP	7.2%	2.9%	2.1%
Average 10-year yield	2.9%	5.2%	3.2%
Annual money growth as % of GDP	1.7%	0.3%	3.3%
Change in total debt as % of GDP	−84%	−249%	−34%

(*Source:* Bridgewater Associates and Global Financial Data, 2012.)

investments. Such a reflation strategy was used in the United States in the 1930s and the United Kingdom in the 1940s. It is notable from Table 3.1 that the total debt-to-GDP ratio falls by 30 to 80 percent, while bond yields are low and the GDP deflator, a measure of inflation, is higher. It is an effective way to stealthily liquidate government debt through paydown and refinancing at lower than normal interest rates. These low rates would not be possible if commercial banks were not required to hold government debt via regulation (Basel III) as part of a capital buffer. Central banks in major developed economies actively pursued the reflation strategy from 2009 onward, which intensified when the terms of chairmen Ben Bernanke of the Federal Reserve and Mervyn King of the Bank of England were coming to an end. A "legacy dividend" was paid by these chairmen to push their monetary policy strategy into "hyper-reflation" to achieve positive economic outcomes in order to leave a legacy of success. It could also be called a bailout by the central banks under cover of large-scale debt deleveraging that depressed nominal growth rates. This growth "depression" is used as an argument by central banks to achieve the objectives of their single or dual mandates.

Bail-in and Bailout Mechanisms

Nouriel Roubini famously discussed the issue of "bail-ins versus bailouts" (i.e., how the private sector could get involved to come up with the right crisis resolution). This is otherwise known as private sector involvement (PSI) and has been cited as the most controversial item in the debate on the reform of the international financial architecture. After several emerging market debt crises in the 1980s and the Greek crisis of 2009 to 2012, there has been a broad agreement among the G20 and the IMF on measures for crisis prevention. There has been much less agreement on measures for crisis resolution. The problem has been characterized in the media in quite different ways: bail-in, burden sharing, private sector involvement, and constructive engagement. The main issue in a PSI is what to do when there is a crisis and an external financing gap (i.e., a large current account deficit).

Roubini defines three options:

1. A big "bailout" in the form of an official support package covering the financing gap
2. A full bail-in of private investors through debt rescheduling, restructuring, reduction, and reprofiling
3. A combination of official financing, PSI, and policy adjustment by the crisis country

The trade-off between how much bail-in is needed relative to bailouts given an external financing gap implies that if one is less available, the need for the other is greater. In a "constructive engagement," the balance between bail-in and bailout has led to small amounts of IMF financing and no or limited coercive forms of PSI. There is circularity at work here. A smaller IMF package may imply relying more on PSI in some coercive form. On the other hand, less coercive PSI means a need for more official financing.

Private Sector Involvement in the 1980s, 1990s, and 2000s

The 1980s developing countries' debt crises had their own specific types of PSI. These consisted of suspension of payments on syndicated bank loans, concerted loans rollovers, new private money, and eventually debt reduction through the Brady plan. As the evolution of the PSI happened, instruments were changed from syndicated medium- to long-term bank loans to shorter-term loans. Creditors saw changes in terms of geographical dispersion and composition in terms of type of private debtors in addition to sovereign debtors. Over time, the challenge was to restructure syndicated bank loans, sovereign and private bonds, and short-term interbank lines. A PSI was not as easy as some thought at the initiation of a restructuring. In particular, such restructuring became impossible in the absence of Collective Action Clauses (CACs) when bonds were held by thousands of creditors, namely those classified as "retail investors." Other hurdles often mentioned are collective action problems of coordinating many different creditors; large number of banks with different interests; holdout problems; and, as Roubini describes, "nonhomogeneous syndicated loans" restructured into more homogeneous bonds or loans. History has shown, however, that sovereign bond restructurings were possible even without CACs (e.g., in Pakistan, Ukraine, Russia, Ecuador, and Argentina). Mostly, debt crises were addressed with a combination of partial bailouts and bail-ins rather than large international bailouts. What changed, too, was that the rationale for a PSI became more straightforward. In the event of a crisis, public sector support cannot fully fill the external financing gap even after a significant fiscal consolidation. When "exceptional financing" would not be feasible because of creditor and debtor "moral hazard" issues, the need for "appropriate" PSI was typically sought. Such was the case in Greece during the height of the European debt crisis in 2011.

Modern-Day Private Sector Involvement: Greece

In May 2011, former European Central Bank (ECB) council member Bini Smaghi said that the Greek government and banks had to look into a "Vienna initiative" for Greek bond holdings. The idea of a "voluntary roll-over" caught on with EU policymakers, specifically those from the Nordic region, who stood pat on private sector contributions in future bailouts. And so the PSI was born, first via the "French proposal" (for French banks) and then via a formal version by the Institute of International Finance at the European Union July 2011 Summit. The idea was to swap existing Greek bonds for new

bonds that would fall under international law ("U.K. law") and have
CACs. These clauses allow for a more "orderly" restructuring process
via majority voting. The PSI swap proposals put forward were complex, but in general, they entailed a 50 percent notional write-down
of total outstanding Greek government debt, excluding the Greek
bond holdings of the ECB. The 50 percent write-down was later
adjusted to 53.5 percent and broken down into 31.5 percent of a
new 10- to 30-year Greek bond and 15 percent payment in the form
of cash and T-bills. The specifics of the PSI were tweaked numerous
times during the negotiation, with moving targets for the coupon on
the new bonds (ranged from 5.5 to 3.65 percent); the assumed "exit
yield" (the discount rate for new bonds), first at 9 percent and later
at 12 percent; and a "sweetener" in the form of short-term bills. The
combination of the new bonds and cash yielded a net present value
(NPV) of the PSI swap. The NPV is a value that essentially expresses
the total price of the package the investors would get in exchange
for their existing Greek bonds. In July 2011, the NPV was 79 cents
for every 100 of Greek bonds. By March 2012, that value became
25 cents for every 100 of Greek bonds. That implies a haircut that
was originally around 21 percent (also stated officially in the EU July
2011 statement), went to 50 percent (stated in the EU October 2011
statement), and eventually ended up at 75 percent. When these haircuts were stated officially, the market caught on, and a "bond price
convergence" between 2- and 30-year maturities happened. This is
depicted in Figure 3.4 on page 77, where the historical PSI value or
haircut (100 − NPV) is plotted against 2- and 30-year bond prices
of Greece. This graph shows how coercive a PSI process can become
when officials start meddling with the proposed haircut.

A big obstacle and unknown during the PSI process was the investors' "participation rate." The IMF debt sustainability analysis in 2011
showed that to achieve a 120 percent debt-to-GDP ratio under certain growth assumptions, at least a 90 percent or higher participation

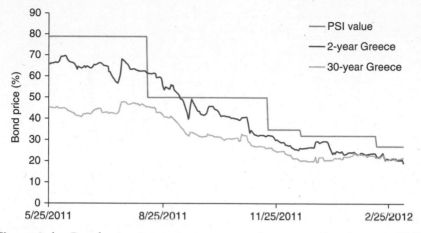

Figure 3.4 Bond price convergence versus private sector involvement (PSI) value history. PSI value is 100 − net present value of the PSI.

(*Source:* Bloomberg, Institute of International Finance.)

rate was needed. Another sticking point was how the ECB was going to participate. The ECB Greek bond holdings (approximately 45 to 50 billion purchased at 75 to 85 cents on the dollar in 2010, according to primary dealer surveys) would not participate in the PSI. Rating agency Standard & Poor's judged that as a result of the ECB actions, the ECB's status as a creditor had changed to senior. As a result, the ECB's Greek bonds were senior to existing creditors, and this might have created a new vision of how central bank creditor status could play out in other future debt restructurings. Investors closely looked at the PSI value of the Greek bonds. At a PSI NPV of 25 to 27 cents, the implied discount yield was 12 to 13 percent. This yield had a range, however, which most market participants estimated to be 12 to 17 percent based on certain growth assumptions. Figure 3.5 on page 78 shows at different exit yields what the value of the PSI NPV could have been.

The Greek PSI completion yielded some results worth paying attention to. The official target was to write down 53.5 percent

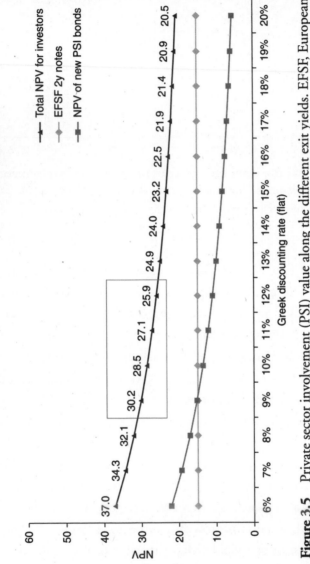

Figure 3.5 Private sector involvement (PSI) value along the different exit yields. EFSF, European Financial Stability Facility; NPV, net present value.

(*Source:* BNP Paribas Research.)

or 110 billion in Greek bonds. Because the PSI was a "voluntary" exchange, the "participation rate" was crucial to reach a 110 billion target of existing bonds being rolled over into new bonds. The end result of the PSI was a total participation rate of 95.7 percent that consented to amend their Greek bond holdings to new terms. Notable was the holdout investor percentage. That was greater for Greek bonds that fell under U.K. law and had CACs. A reason was that in some of the bonds, specific funds built a majority position that could block the voting on changes. One of those was a floating rate note denominated in euros that matured in May 2012. The holders of that bond were paid 100 on 440 million of holdings, but creditors in other Greek bonds under U.K. law had to accept a haircut of 75 percent.

Another case was the Greek government bond that paid a 4.3 percent coupon and matured on March 15, 2012, for a total of 14.3 billion euros notional outstanding. Because the ECB holdings were exempted from the PSI, it was revealed that the ECB held 4.6 billion of the Greek government bond maturing on March 15, 2012. Because the ECB was a preferred creditor, it received 100 when the bond was redeemed. The remaining notional of the bond (9.7 billion) that was in the hands of private creditors received the "PSI package." The net result was that these creditors received only 25 cents. The way the ECB was paid 100 was through loans from the European Financial Stability Facility to Greece. Because Greece received its tranche payment in exchange for tough reforms and fiscal measures, part of the loan was used to redeem the ECB Greek bond holdings. The profit the ECB made on the bonds because it bought them at a discount was paid in dividends by the national central banks to their respective governments over time. Based on the key capital percentage distribution, even the Greek central bank would pay a small part of that profit back to the Greek government. This was a unique feature of the Greek PSI process.

Official Sector Involvement

When the Greek PSI was completed, the realization set in that the notional write-down of Greek debt was not enough. This led to a revisiting of Greece's long-term debt sustainability in the fall of 2012. The European Union and IMF officials "clashed" over how to get Greece back on track given its large mountain of debt (approximately 310 billion euros, according to Euro Stat). After the PSI, about two thirds of Greek debt was held by the European Union and the IMF, consisting of bilateral loans and loans from the European Financial Stability Fund. Because Greece's GDP continued to shrink in 2012, the debt-to-GDP ratio rose to 145 percent, and the trajectory showed a worsening to 195 percent by 2020. The IMF pressed EU officials to take a "haircut" on the loans, which became known as official sector involvement (OSI). Germany, the Netherlands, and several others did not want to take a haircut on the principal of the loans but rather opted for a reduction in interest owed, extending the maturity of the loans, and a buyback of outstanding restructured debt. The debt buyback was a particular focus. At an initial price range estimate of 28 cents to 35 cents, the holders of the restructured Greek bonds were faced with another haircut of 65 to 72 percent from par. A simple calculation based on the original notional write-down (53.5 percent) during the PSI said that the buyback resulted in an additional notional write-down of 25 percent. And as leaked reports showed, there was a "fudge" in Greece's targeted debt-to-GDP ratios, where the debt-to-GDP numbers were worse than what was communicated officially. That implied that more haircuts eventually may come in the future, potentially by both OSI and PSI.

The Greek debt buyback was said to be "voluntary." The Greek banks that owned about 17 to 20 billion euros in Greek bonds were strong-armed by Greek officials to accept the buyback offer. And they were because their participation in the final result was a 100 percent. Another issue was the "regional investor dispersion." Greek restructured bonds were held by Cypriot, French, German, and Belgian banks. The dispersion was an issue during the PSI because each party had specific ideas about the bond exchange and the PSI NPV. The buyback revisited that issue through how each party saw the optimal buyback price. That in turn influenced the "participation rate." As expectations over investor participation worsened, the more uncertain the final results became. Like during the PSI, the rating agencies judged that the debt buyback was coercive. They placed Greek restructured debt on "selective default." In turn, the ECB had to reject that collateral temporarily until the buyback was completed. Unlike during the PSI, the collateral issue was of less concern to the markets. One of the worst parts of the PSI process was how the haircut was openly communicated. That adverse communication spilled over negatively to other European peripheral bond markets. Fortunately, the debt buyback did not work that way. However, as talks went on, the market drove up the buyback price range, resulting in more money being provided by Germany and other countries to finance the buyback. The buyback was financed by T-bills issued by the European Financial Stability Fund. The European Union eventually ended up buying 31 billion in restructured bonds. That resulted in shaving about 3 to 5 percent off the Greek debt-to-GDP ratio. The other measures (interest rate cut, maturity extension) had about half the effect on the debt-to-GDP ratio (approximately 2.7 percent) compared with what the buyback achieved.

The debt buyback result was important for the EU and the IMF. Because it was a "success," the likelihood of a repeat if Greece were to slide off track again remained high. The Greek case teaches investors that a haircut is an easy way for public officials to meet fiscal objectives. Investors who benefited from the Greek buyback were those who purchased Greek restructured bonds when the distress about Greece's exit increased in May 2012. The bondholders of the restructured bonds, on the other hand, had to take another haircut. Bond investors who bought the Greek restructured bonds after the buyback may still face a notional write-down even if they make potential capital gains. The process of haircuts can linger for years, as the case of Argentina has shown.

Recent Case: Argentina

Argentina has been struggling with bondholders for a number of years. Their case is about holdouts that refused to cooperate in debt exchanges. It led to another showdown between Argentina, the U.S. Court of Appeals, and investors in late 2012. Investors in Argentina's restructured bonds opposed a judicial order that required the country to pay interest on the defaulted debt, which threatened their rights to receive payments. These were bondholders that held restructured bonds the country issued in 2005 and 2010 after Argentina defaulted on sovereign debt in 2001. In November 2012, U.S. District Judge Thomas Griesa in New York issued an injunction requiring the country to pay $1.3 billion owed to holders of defaulted bonds when it makes payments on the restructured debt. Bond investors that held the restructured bonds argued that the injunction was unlawful and unconstitutional. Their view was that such an injunction would infringe the rights of "innocent" third-party creditors. The Argentinean government said it does not intend to pay holders of the defaulted debt who opted not to accept the country's exchange offers of 25 to 29 cents on the dollar, according to the court's filing. The country's law also prohibits the payment of defaulted debt, the exchange bondholders argued. If the injunction was not vacated, it became almost "certain" that either the country would fail to pay the exchange bonds or the payments would be frozen. Other parties, such as the trustees for restructured Argentine bonds, said that Judge Griesa's ruling would force a violation of bond contracts. Judge Griesa ordered trustee banks to help carry out the ruling by withholding funds from restructured bondholders until Argentina pays the old debt. Trustee banks were obligated under contract to pay restructured bondholders. This led to further conflict and ongoing litigation. And so, as the Argentinean and Belize precedents have also shown, price haggling, cajoling, and arm twisting are parts of a debt write-down negotiation. These elements make it difficult to achieve debt sustainability. In the process, the holdouts get more severe, which can lead to further coercive haircuts. These lead to litigation and may even result in technical default on the part of the government in question.

A Cypriot Parallel Deposit

When the Greek PSI was completed in March 2012, the losses were steep for banks in Cyprus. Holdings amounting to 5 billion in Greek government bonds (10 percent of total bank assets), once purchased above 100, were cut in value by 75 percent. This required the Cypriot banks to be recapitalized. As a result, Cyprus was the fifth European country to receive an international bailout. The complexity of the Cyprus case was that the banks held large foreign deposits, namely coming from Russians who sought Cyprus out as a tax haven. Cyprus' corporate tax rate of 10 percent attracted so many deposits that bank assets swelled to 8 times GDP. When the bailout was negotiated in March 2013, depositors were going to take part in the bailout, given the size and scope of their financing of Cypriot banks. Initially, insured depositors were asked to take losses. This caused havoc in markets, as many saw this as a dangerous precedent. Quickly realizing that this was a mistake, the European leaders decided to have only uninsured depositors (those holding more than 100,000 in the bank) bailed in, alongside the subordinated bond holders and equity holders.

The key lesson of the Cypriot case was that in a bailout, essentially no one is really "safe," not even depositors. This affected creditors' behavior with regard to the capital structure. Deposits provide an important service to an economy. Without deposits, a fractional reserve system could not function. Risk to an economy occurs when deposit holders decide to run, as this can paralyze financial systems and cripple economies. Deposit runs have often been at the base of bank failures. The situation in Cyprus didn't cause a widespread deposit run due to capital controls. Those controls, however, were unique in the European Monetary Union, since no other country was subjected to such restrictions. The Cyprus case as well as the Greek, Spanish, Dutch, and Irish bank bailouts all had one thing in common: bailing in revealed that creditors could expect a low recovery rate of about 20 to 25 percent. This recovery value has set expectations among creditors as to what may be expected in future shared bailouts. And even these individual cases are specified as unique, as collectively the bailouts were subjugated by the European Commission. Dutch Finance Minister Dijsselbloem saw Cyprus as a "template," and markets took strong note that the sanctity of deposits had been changed.

Haircuts applied to different groups of creditors spared several asset classes, such as senior unsecured and covered bonds, as well as bonds issued by the ESM and EFSF. The latter finance bailout loans, and so to see haircuts on those would be quite unlikely. Now that creditors in Europe have an idea of what the "template" for future bailouts could look like, ESM bond yields may serve as a benchmark to price risk premiums. In fact, European senior and subfinancial CDS widened by 60 basis points during the Cyprus bailout. The risk of other PSI type solutions resurfaced as Slovenian bond yields shot up 200 basis points. This market reaction was not too dissimilar to what happened when Ireland, Portugal, and Greece lost market access shortly before they were bailed out. The market has perhaps taken notice that ESM-funded bailouts means applying the ESM risk premium to other credits. All insured and uninsured deposits run parallel globally and pose a medium-term idiosyncratic risk. When such risks get elevated, the effects could be felt through indirect tax methods like international trade tariffs, negative real interest rates, and capital account restrictions.

These measures alter the capital structures of countries, and Europe is taking the forefront in the process. The result is that the universe of safe assets (AAA rated) could shrink further. In the case of Europe, what may be left as "safe" or "risk free" are the bonds issued by the ESM. As bail-ins and bailouts continue, it would be natural for ESM bonds to take on a stronger role as a common bond, under which the debt burden is appropriately shared, including uninsured deposits.

A Transformation

Despite the debt buyback, the long-term sustainability of Greece's debt kept the debate of haircuts alive through PSI, OSI, or combined and continued to set an example for what a sovereign debt restructuring could look like for an advanced economy. The Greek government bond market was also the first market to undergo a "transformation." When the ESM became operational in October 2012, it also meant that every new government bond issue with a maturity of 1 year or longer would have CACs starting in 2013. The Greek government bond market became a "proxy" for what the future of the European government bond market could look like. The proxy indicated two things: (1) the initial idea of what the risk premium should be between bonds that have CACs and those that do not and (2) a premium of a second kind of PSI as Greek debt sustainability remained in question.

Collective Action Clauses

Collective Action Clauses enable creditors to pass a qualified majority decision to agree to a legally binding change in the terms of a bond contract. When a majority of bondholders agrees, such changes are binding on others. A change in terms could be a maturity extension, a cut in the coupon interest, or a "haircut" in the notional value of a bond. Under the "U.K. law," a sovereign debt restructuring typically requires a 75 percent majority to vote in favor. A democratic voting process has been viewed as a benefit to bondholders rather than having to face a coercive change of their bonds. The CACs could allow for an orderly, standardized restructuring process for sovereign bonds. CACs originated from an initiative by the Group of 10 major industrialized countries in 2002 to promote expeditious procedures for orderly restructurings during crises. Because a majority of foreign sovereign debt is governed by a handful of jurisdictions, the G10 workgroup put forward an agreement on a general set of provisions suitable for sovereign debt. The objectives were to foster early dialogue and coordination and communication among creditors. The CACs were the most critical components to provide flexibility in agreements to be reached regarding restructuring in collective interest. In addition to a qualified voting majority (75 percent), the workgroup judged that a minimum quorum of the outstanding principal would be required, typically 25 to 50 percent at a bondholder's meeting. As of today, there is not a full standardization among sovereign jurisdictions related to majority voting and quorum. For example, in Japan, a supermajority resolution can be adopted by two thirds of the voting rights present or represented at a bondholders' meeting. Most international sovereign debt markets are under Japanese, German, or New York law. In general, these fall under the denominator "local law," where the sovereign issuers can impose changes to their debt without majority bondholder consent.

There is also a distinction between bonds issued under the U.K. and New York law; bonds issued under New York law require a unanimous consent, unlike bonds under U.K. law, which typically have CACs and do not require unanimous votes. In the wake of the 1994 to 1995 Mexico "Tequila crisis" and Argentina's 2001 restructuring, the call grew to include CACs in sovereign debt issues. And so by 2003, when Mexico issued the first bond with CACs that required a 75 percent majority voting, the transformation began in emerging markets, as depicted in Figure 3.6 on page 87.

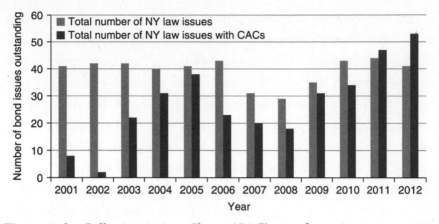

Figure 3.6 Collective Action Clause (CAC) transformation in emerging markets sovereign debt markets.

(*Source:* Gulati & Bradley. "Collective Action Clauses for the Eurozone: An Empirical Analysis," Duke University Papers, 2011.)

There is a lively academic debate on the pros and cons of CACs. As mentioned, the main benefit of CACs is that without such clauses, a distressed sovereign would either default or request a bailout. The official sector has encouraged the use of CACs to alleviate the need for taxpayer funds, but also to prevent the "holdouts problem." Past sovereign debt restructurings were accompanied by a bankruptcy process that was not formally organized. At times, this has encouraged a specific group of bondholders to hold out on agreeing to a change in payment terms. The standard practice for a long time has been for bondholder rights to be individual rather than collective, with any modification of the bond contract having to be negotiated with each bondholder individually. The complexity arises because even when a majority of bondholders agrees to the restructuring terms, an individual bondholder could refuse to do so, thus frustrating the attempted reorganization. When the number of bondholders is large and represents a wide variety of investors that are geographically dispersed, the holdout problem can become severe. More specifically, a certain group of investors could have had the intentional purpose of investing in the debt issue for the sole purpose of holding out and demanding a disproportionate payment in exchange for their bonds. In light of the holdout problem, different types of CACs have been applied. The most common is the "modification CAC," in which a minimum vote based on a quorum allows for modification of terms. The requirement can be as high as 100 percent (unanimous vote) or as low as 18 percent (if the quorum is below 50 percent). Another type is "disenfranchise-ment CAC," which can bar certain bondholders from voting. Certain bonds under New York or U.K. law have explicit provisions that dis-enfranchise bonds owned or controlled by the issuers. Others allow the issuer's central bank to vote; and still others are silent as to who can vote, suggesting that the issuer has the right to vote on its own bonds. Increasingly since 2003, such disenfranchisement clauses have been included in New York and U.K. law's emerging market bonds' CAC as depicted in Figure 3.7.

There is also a kind of CAC that has aggregation provisions. This provision extends further than the 75 percent majority vote to deter holdout investors. The aggregation specifies provisions that govern

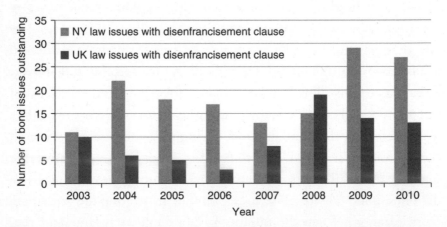

Figure 3.7 Collective Action Clauses with disenfranchisement clauses.

(*Source:* Gulati & Bradley. "Collective Action Clauses for the Eurozone: An Empirical Analysis," Duke University Papers, 2011.)

modification of the terms of all bonds outstanding. Other important aspects are "acceleration" and "reverse acceleration." In the event of a default, individual creditors could accelerate all future payments owed to them to the present time. To avoid this element to further accentuate the holdout problem, since 2002, both U.K. and New York law issues contain acceleration provisions requiring a 25 percent vote before there could be an acceleration of payments. By 2010, acceleration provisions were used by more than 50 percent of the issuers under both U.K. and New York law according to research by Bradley and Gulati. In a reverse acceleration provision, a 50 percent vote of bondholders would be able to reverse the acceleration clause in the event that a holdout creditor would own a 25 percent block of a particular bond. This provision is meant to preempt an acquisition of a block vote. In general, most issues that have acceleration provisions also contain a reverse acceleration. There are a few other provisions such as the bondholder committee, wherein a representative body would coordinate negotiations between creditors and debtors. The G10 workgroup on CACs judged that such committees could be formed with the consent of bondholders with more than 50 percent of the outstanding principal. Other aspects of the bondholder meetings include whether they could be mandatory. This means that a vote to change the payment terms has to take place at a physical meeting.

Because insertion of CACs is mainstream in emerging markets issuance, such will be the case in European government bond markets as of 2013. The question on investors' minds becomes whether such CACs would have a meaningful impact on the valuation of a government bond risk premium. The academic literature has been divided on whether CACs reduce costs for issuers and translate into higher or lower risk premiums. The most profound effect would be the modification CACs based on majority voting and a quorum. Barry Eichengreen found that yield differences could be explained between bonds with CACs of more and less creditworthy issuers. A backdrop is the flexibility allowed by creditors for a country to restructure its debt. Bondholders would want the restructuring process to be as easy as possible. When a country has the most need to establish credibility, specific debt payment rules are needed to convince creditors.

Empirical analysis by Gulati and Bradley suggests that the introduction of CACs after 2004 for lower-quality issuing countries was associated with lower bond spreads. The basic reason was that restructurings are easier and less costly when vote thresholds for payment modification are lower. Gulati and Bradley revealed further that acceleration provisions in lower-rated, less creditworthy issuers are significantly correlated with lower-risk premiums for bonds issued under both New York and U.K. law. Logically, more creditworthy issuers who can freely borrow on their own currency under their domestic law enjoy confidence from creditors, and those creditors do not impose significant contractual restrictions. Extrapolated to the future, the CAC attachment to German government bonds may not necessarily always make their yields lower than those of U.S. Treasuries. A narrowing relative yield difference may occur for lower-rated issuers such as Italy if creditors are willing to give them more flexible terms to ameliorate the risk of holdout investors in a future restructuring. That is to say that the CAC may not per se imply a higher chance of restructurings in Europe. There are many different cases in which differentiation among CACs, the time of original issuance, market depth of liquidity, and currency volatility play distinct roles in determining the yield demanded by investors. CACs moving from emerging markets into developed markets is a significant development, however. The clauses not only determine the outcomes of a restructuring process but may also lead to further credit rating and liquidity migration among emerging and developed capital markets. Over time, as CACs see further standardization in terms of different provisions, it could also standardize global bond markets, at least in terms of what investors can expect from a bankruptcy process.

Collective Action Clauses in Europe

On February 2, 2012, a modification of the Lisbon Treaty was established. It would enable the ESM to come into effect after the treaty change was signed by all 17 euro area member states. In paragraph 3 of Article 12 of the treaty, it was stated that as of January 1, 2013, CACs would be included in all new euro area government debt securities with an original stated maturity of more than 1 year. In this way, it was ensured that the legal impact across member states would be identical. The Economic and Financial Committee developed and approved the European model CACs. For the CACs two types of modifications were distinguished. These are modifications of the borrowing conditions that can be made with approval of the majority of the bondholders in a bondholder meeting. There is a reserved matter modification that involves the modification of a bond's most relevant terms and conditions. These could be, for example, reductions in principal or interest payable on a bond. There can also be changes in the dates on which these payments must be made. It is obvious that if these modifications were to be made, they would require the highest level of consent by all bondholders. There is also a nonreserved matter modification. This means a modification of a bond's terms and conditions that are deemed of lower importance. In broad terms, these are any modification, amendment, supplement, or waiver of the trust indenture or the terms and conditions of the bonds. The modification would require a lower level of consent of bondholders, as it legally does not constitute a reserved matter. When CACs come into effect, a modification may be proposed in different ways. They may be related to a single bond, called a single-series modification. They could also relate to more than one bond at the same time, known as a cross-series modification. There are different thresholds for approval that apply to single-series and cross-series modifications. In all events, a proposed modification will always require the issuer's consent. Modifications, if approved, are binding for all bondholders. The introduction of the European model CACs will not affect any European government bonds issued before January 1, 2013. In March 2011, the European Council concluded that all euro area member states should be allowed, under agreed-upon conditions, to reopen debt issuances outstanding on the date of the CAC's mandatory introduction to preserve market liquidity. Member states agreed that up to 45 percent of the total face amount of all central government issuance in 2013 may be raised via reopening (i.e., in securities that do not include CACs).

Market participants and primary dealers have had mixed feelings about the introduction of CACs. Some view it as "window dressing," saying the CAC will not really bring stability for European sovereign debt because it is not seen as an "insurance" against default. Others see practical issues such as the technicalities surrounding government bond strips (fungible) and delivery of bonds in a bond futures contract. In the fall of 2010, investors saw the introduction of CACs as a negative. The issue of subordination was frequently debated because government bonds with CACs would be treated differently during a restructuring from those without. The Greek PSI showed that was not the case; however, the incentive to hold out on CAC bonds was greater than on bonds without CACs. There was also a view that CACs would make it easier for European governments to opt for restructuring if debt-to-GDP targets could not be met. The history of emerging market restructurings has shown that it is not always a given that governments get away with restructuring easily when their debt has CACs attached. Holdout investors could become a severe problem.

The "Holdout Problem"

When the number of bondholders is large, diverse, and geographically dispersed, a holdout problem has at times become severe. A holdout investor has therefore been called a "vulture creditor" who buys

Table 3.2   The Triggering of Collective Action Clauses Under U.K. and New York Law

	Argentina 2001, 2005	Uruguay 2003	Dominica 2004	Seychelles 2009	Greece 2012
Restructuring duration (mos)	42	2	15	19	11
Haircut (%)	76.30%	9.80%	54%	56.20%	79%
CACs triggered	Yes	Yes	Yes	Yes	Yes
Holdouts (%)	24%	7%	28%	16%	3%
Participation rate (%)	76%	93%	72%	89%	95%
Litigation cases	>100	1	1	0	0

(*Source:* Ratna Sahay, IMF Research (2012): "A Survey of Experiences with Emerging Market Sovereign Debt Restructurings.")

debt at a deep discount on the secondary market but sues the sovereign issuer for full debt repayment. In past emerging markets debt restructurings (Table 3.2), in the majority of restructuring cases, CACs were applied to original or new bonds. In some cases, such as Uruguay in 2003, CACs helped a swift restructuring, according to the IMF. In other examples, such as Argentina in 2005 and Dominica in 2004, CACs could not prevent a severe holdout problem partly because of a wide geographical dispersion of creditors. Even the most recent restructuring in Greece saw holdouts on its international bond—a floating rate note maturing in May 2012—despite a high investor participation rate of more than 90 percent.

A key reason for holdouts in the case of Argentina was that after its 2001 financial crisis, bondholders and the IMF criticized Argentina, which decided to suddenly act on its own after several years of negotiations. Argentina suspended its agreement with the IMF and filed for a one-time unilateral offer with the Securities and Exchange Commission to settle with creditors. In 2005, Argentina held a debt exchange for a total of $81 billion in outstanding debt. Of that amount, about

24 percent, or $19.6 billion, was "held out" by investors who did not participate in the tender. The holdout creditors pursued litigation to force repayment that resulted in Argentina's being precluded from borrowing in capital markets until the defaulted bonds are repaid or restructured.

In the case of Dominica, three specific financial institutions held out but were gradually convinced to accept the original exchange offer. Table 3.2 demonstrates that whenever the amount of holdout investors is large, the haircut and the duration of the restructuring process can be, too. Not surprisingly, factors such as these tend to depress sovereign bond prices.

As Figure 3.8 on page 95 shows, bond prices tend to fall beginning about 10 months before restructuring and continue to decline for about another 6 months, then prices tend to rally. This pattern may result from (1) a fall in sovereign ratings as restructuring places bonds on a temporary default status, (2) a decline in the discount rate assumed, and (3) expectations of an improved debt-sustainability trajectory and debt-recovery rates after the restructuring. This pattern does not always hold, however: ongoing litigation in Argentina and an uncertain economic outlook in Greece depressed liquidity in their bond markets, preventing for a while a rebound in bond prices. Noteworthy is that when the discussion of debt buybacks as part of the OSI needed to bring the Greek debt-to-GDP ratio back on track began, Greek bond prices significantly recovered.

Conclusion: Difficult Choices

Sovereign debt restructurings are unique and unpredictable. In general, the longer restructuring lasts, the greater the uncertainty for the investor. Investors have to carefully assess the terms of debt exchange, the number of holdouts, and the risk of potentially different treatment for official creditors. In addition, analysis of the debt composition is

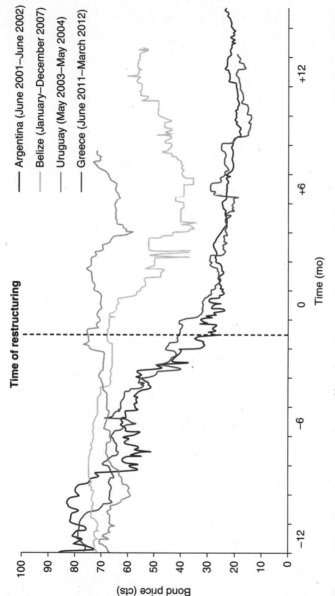

Figure 3.8 How restructurings affect bond prices. Bonds used: Argentina 11.75% 6/15/2015 (USD denominated); Belize 8.5% 2/2029 (USD denominated); Uruguay 7.875% 1/2033 (USD denominated); GGB 3.9% 7/2013 (EUR denominated); and GGB 2% 2/2023 (EUR denominated). Data used are for 12 months before and 12 months after restructuring (except for Greece, which is 6 months since restructuring).

(*Source:* Bloomberg.)

essential to determine the share of foreign currency, floating rate, and short-term debt. On balance, the introduction of CACs in European government bond markets in 2013 has caused mixed feelings among investors. The history of emerging markets and Greece shows that there are no shortcuts: Investors must continue to be selective and use bottom-up analysis to assess credit risks. It is a striking change from the pre–financial crisis era, when most developed market government bonds were regarded as "risk free." Connected to that thesis are the debt speed bumps major advanced economies were running into. The United States struggled in 2011 to reach an agreement to extend its debt ceiling, almost leading to a technical default on U.S. Treasury debt. The debate revealed a significant polarization of the political spectrum that failed to reach a comprehensive solution to bring the U.S. deficit onto a sustainable path. This resulted in a downgrade of U.S. Treasury debt by Standard & Poor's that specifically cited concerns about the political will to tackle structural issues such as entitlement spending. In 2012, the United States was confronted with the "fiscal cliff," a combination of expiring tax cuts from the Bush era, required defense spending reductions, and other items. Whether one looks at this example, the discussion about Greece's debt sustainability, or political debates about austerity elsewhere, they all have in common the difficult choices that had to be made. Because those choices are politically "unbearable," they continue to be put off, or, as the market oxymoron says, "kick the can down the road." This kind of strategy, despite overhaul with CACs, has created more risk complexities around the risk-free rate.

Part II

Investment Implications

Chapter 4

Some Quantification

The risk-free rate was traditionally characterized by high liquidity, low default, and perceived safety. That idea has changed. Investors now have to analyze credit risk attributes of the risk-free rate, something that was not done before. These attributes can be broken down into two major categories, fundamental and technical. Fundamental speaks to a host of economic, country, and debt risk metrics. Technical factors are related to liquidity, default, credit, and currency risk. Underneath are subsectors such as policy, social-political, financial repression, and liquidity traps. When incorporating these into a framework, the picture becomes more complex as more types of risk are added, as shown in Figure 4.1 on page 100.

The following sections demonstrate a risk premium estimate of each component. It has to be said that these are estimates based on *basic* analysis, but the purpose is to demonstrate what each of the factors cited in Figure 4.1 means when thinking of a change in the risk-free rate. It's a *conceptual* framework. The identified risks are real, however, and are a direct result of the significant changes that have taken place since 2008.

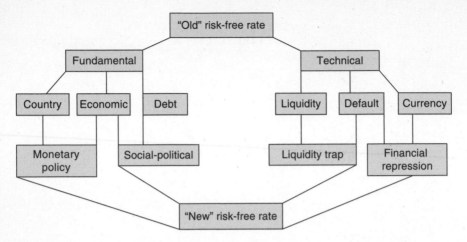

Figure 4.1   Framework to distinguish risk components of the risk-free rate.

Fundamental Aspects of Risk Premium in the Risk-Free Rate

Structural economic impediments such as persistent high unemployment, high productivity, lower potential growth, and greater inflation volatility have become more commonplace. In addition, there are deteriorating trends in demographics, ratios of debt to gross domestic product (GDP), and the balance of payments. This brings about the psychology of risk aversion and social-political rejection, which are feeding back into the economic risks such as those described in Chapter 2. Monetary policy having a proactive role causes manipulation of risk-free rates. In general, the primary risk associated with bonds is interest rate risk. Say an investor purchases a Treasury bond that has a 10-year maturity with a coupon and yield of 2 percent. Mathematically, the duration of the 10-year bond is about 9.1 years, and during that time, an investor can earn 2 percent. Yet a significant amount of fundamental and technical risk factors is embedded in that yield. To start with, for example, these factors include country risk associated with politics, infrastructure, population, and financial regulation, but also default and currency. New York

Table 4.1 Country Risk Premiums

Region	Total (%)
Africa	3.72
Asia	3.57
Australia and New Zealand	0.00
Caribbean	4.52
Central and South America	4.85
Eastern Europe and Russia	3.94
Financial Center	0.00
Middle East	2.03
North America	0.00
Western Europe	1.90
Grand total	**3.34**

(*Source:* Damodaran, Aswath. Country risk premiums, 2012. Available at http://people.stern.nyu.edu/ adamodar/pc/datasets/ctrypremJune2012.xls.)

University Stern School of Business's Aswath Damodaran has done work in estimating country risk premiums. His "basic" formula for country risk is to multiply the credit default swap (CDS) spread times the ratio of equity market volatility divided by bond market volatility. When using this methodology, the country risk premiums for major developed countries can be calculated as shown in Table 4.1.

It is notable that the country risk on this basis is low for the developed countries (United States, Europe, Australia) and high for emerging countries (Asia, Africa, Central and South America). Euromoney, a financial markets survey company, has specialized in a country risk index titled Euromoney Country Risk (ECR) Index. The methodology is a weighted index determined by six categories. These are the political risk (30 percent weighting), economic performance (30 percent weighting), and structural assessment (10 percent weighting) of a country. The ECR also uses quantitative values such as debt indicators (10 percent

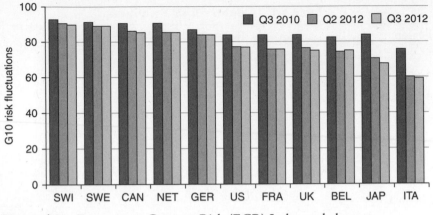

Figure 4.2   Euromoney Country Risk (ECR) Index and change.
(*Source:* http://www.euromoneycountryrisk.com.)

weighting), credit ratings (10 percent weighting), and access to bank finance and capital markets (10 percent weighting). Based on their latest readings in the fall of 2012, the ECR index shows the following score and change from 2 years earlier (Figure 4.2). Whereas a fall in the index implies an increased country risk, notably, the ECR indexes of the United States, the United Kingdom, Japan, and France have fallen. The short-term interest rates—risk-free rates—of these countries are near zero, which would say on the surface that there is little risk. Measures such as the ECR index show that there is country risk. It argues that such risk is *embedded* in the risk-free rate. This is factual, as since 2010, while the interest rates of the United States, the United Kingdom, and Japan have been near zero, their country risk, according to the ECR index in Figure 4.2, has increased.

Another approach is by the Economist Intelligence Unit, which publishes individual country risk indices. Overall, country risk is derived by taking a simple average of the scores for sovereign risk, currency risk, and banking sector risk. Also, these indices consist of a set of risks, such as sovereign risk measured as the risk of default on public,

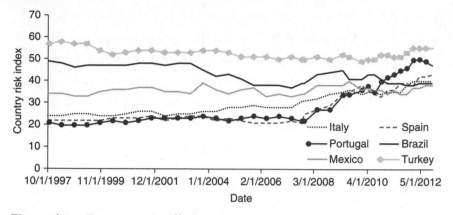

Figure 4.3 Economist Intelligence Unit country risk indices.
(*Source:* Economist Intelligence Unit, Bloomberg.)

domestic, and external debt. The indices also quantify currency, systematic banking crisis, political system, and structural economic indicators risk. Figure 4.3 shows that there is a "convergence" in country risk indices between Italy, Spain, and Portugal on the one hand and Brazil, Mexico, and Turkey on the other. Investors perceive Spain, Italy, and Portugal to be as risky as Brazil, Mexico, and Turkey, even though there are vast differences between the economies. It is a trend that has been intensifying as part of an interest rate convergence between emerging and developed economies. This is happening because certain emerging market economies are maturing, and have seen their sovereign rating upgraded. Those countries therefore experienced high capital inflows.

This is perhaps not surprising; since the country risk indices of these countries are in proximity to one another, so are their interest rates. Portuguese and Turkish government bonds were both trading around 7 percent in 2012. Before 2008, the difference between their yields was as wide as 5 percent. The same can be said of Italy and Spain versus Brazil and Mexico, where bond yields were all close to each other in the area of 5 to 6 percent. This simple example shows how bond yields once perceived as risk free, such as those in Spain and Italy from 2000 to 2008, can at some point face a change of heart by creditors. Related, the level of debt to GDP, a primary surplus or deficit, and projected economic growth all affect how interest rate expectations are formed. When a country runs a primary deficit or surplus, it means after interest expenses are deducted from the total budget. The interest expenses a government incurs are the yields prevailing in the government bond market at which the budget can be financed. A primary surplus or deficit therefore has an impact on the total debt-to-GDP ratio. In addition, projected real GDP influences the primary balance, the debt-to-GDP ratio, and the level of interest rates. And so a dynamic formula to use is to calculate an "equilibrium rate" that incorporates these elements. This equilibrium is the level of interest rates needed to stabilize the debt-to-GDP ratio at the present level. As Table 4.2 shows, many countries need negative interest rates to achieve longer-term sustainability of their debt. If they fail to reach debt sustainability, the current level of bond yields could be far higher. This is what would be the "true" risk-free rate, the difference between the current yield and the equilibrium yield.

The numbers in Table 4.2 show that many countries have bond yields that are too low if their governments were asked to pay off their debt tomorrow. Based on debt and projected growth, interest rates should actually be much higher. In the case of the United States, the United Kingdom, and Japan, a central bank has helped to keep bond yields artificially low. The level of their bond yields masks the growth and debt problems these countries face. Even in the case of countries such as Portugal and Greece, where interest rates have risen dramatically during the European debt crisis as a result of debt aversion, their interest rates are still too low given the worsening debt and growth metrics. In summary, the difference between the "theoretical" equilibrium yield and the current yield represents a risk premium that incorporates debt, economics, and policy. This embedded risk premium stood at a historic high in 2012.

Table 4.2   True Risk-Free Rates*

	Current 10-Year Rate (%)	Equilibrium 10-Year Rate (%)	The "True" Risk-Free Rate (%)
United States	1.75	−4.4	6.15
United Kingdom	1.82	−5.8	7.62
Germany	1.4	−0.3	1.7
Italy	4.5	−2.7	7.2
Spain	5.26	−7.4	12.66
Japan	0.71	−3.30	4.0
Greece	15	−10.26	25.3
Portugal	7.5	−6.75	14.3
Belgium	2.17	−2.67	4.8
Australia	3.16	−1.36	4.5
Mexico	5.5	3.33	2.2
Brazil	8.9	2.32	6.6
China	3.19	10.17	−7.0

*The equilibrium rate is calculated as yield = primary balance/debt-to-GDP (gross domestic product) ratio * 100 + projected real GDP. For example, the 10-year U.S. equilibrium rate = −6.8/107% * 100 + 2% = −4.4%. The "true" risk-free rate for the United States would be 1.75 − (−4.4) = 6.15%. Yield data were taken at the end of December 2012.

(*Sources:* IMF Fiscal Monitor October 2012, IMF World Economic Outlook 2012, and Bloomberg data for generic bond yields.)

Technical Aspects of Risk Premium in the Risk-Free Rate

A bond investor also has to understand what technically drives demand for bonds. The standard items are liquidity and funding. Liquidity can be measured as the difference between where bonds can be sold (the bid side) and can be bought (the offered side); funding is a metric that has several aspects. There is the repurchase financing at which bonds can be lent or borrowed as collateral. This is the "repo market," which reflects financing conditions in different bond markets. There is a distinct difference between funding premium and illiquidity. The latter appears when the threat of sovereign insolvency is caused by rollover risk. On the other hand, diminishing funding premium could exacerbate the risk of sovereign default. Funding remains a major driver for inter-bank liquidity and willingness to accept government bonds onto banks' balance sheets. This premium is not visible in every bond market. In well-developed markets such as those for U.S. Treasuries, U.K. Gilts, German Bunds, and Japanese government bonds (JGBs), there is greater visibility of financing conditions. Default premium, on the other hand, is the CDS market where live prices are made on expectations of a sovereign default. The CDS contract is expressed as a premium where investors can either protect themselves against a default or sell this protection premium if they believe there is a low or no possibility of default. This is the probability of default that is implied by the CDS contract premium and the recovery ratio. This ratio is based on default history across many sovereign markets. Typically the recovery ratio is assumed to be around 40 percent based on historical experience. The percentage means how much an investor can expect to get back from its bond holdings when a government defaults on its debt.

A related issue here is the risk of "convertibility." This is the risk when a bond's currency denomination is converted into another currency. This occurs when a country issues debt in a foreign currency and fails to meet its obligations. At default, the debt is redenominated into the country's local currency. Convertibility risk is hard to quantify, but some exchange rate models published by Rudiger Dornbush and Paul Krugman may provide an answer. Convertibility risk happens through the political process or through a default. Anticipating such events, it could lead to "over-shooting" of sovereign bond yields. This is a reaction by investors when analysis of a sovereign issuer's creditworthiness changes perceptions. Overshooting has been modeled under the assumption that foreign exchange markets are "flexible." The real economy, however, experiences "rigidity" in goods and labor markets. When a sudden change in monetary or fiscal policy happens, the exchange rate reacts instantly, but goods prices and labor wages adjust with a lag. As a result, the exchange rate overshoots its long-run "equilibrium"—purchasing power parity—for a period of time until goods and labor markets adjust. When an exchange rate mechanism is fixed or semipegged, the link between the currency market and bond yields can intensify. By looking at the interest rate parity relationship, this domestic bond yield equals the sum of the foreign yield plus the expected change in the currency. A similar overshooting pattern is present here; countries with low interest rates are perceived to have low default, liquidity, and convertibility risk. Those low interest rates may appear to cover all those risks. That said, low interest rates are not necessarily an insurance against technical risks. In Table 4.3, the different types of risks are shown.

Table 4.3 Technical Aspects: Liquidity, Default Probability, and Convertibility*

	Default Probability (%)	Liquidity (%)	Convertibility (%)
Australia	1.1	0.008	0.02
Brazil	2.2	0.5	0.06
China	1.9	1	0.02
France	2.8	0.005	0.00
Germany	1.2	0.002	0.00
Greece	20	1	0.13
Italy	5.3	0.4	0.03
Japan	1.8	0.001	0.01
Portugal	12.7	1	0.06
Spain	5.6	0.4	0.04
United Kingdom	1	0.003	0.00
United States	0.6	0.001	0.00

*Dornbush measure = domestic yield – foreign yield – expected change in the currency (FX). Expected change in FX: 1 – FX rate 1-year forward rate/FX Spot rate. U.S. yields are taken as foreign yield. All spot and forward exchanges are versus the dollar. Default probability is implied from sovereign credit default swap (CDS).
(*Source:* Bloomberg, Deutsche Bank.)

Financial Repression Premium

In her extensive research, Carmen Reinhart has shown how financial repression is applied in the modern day. There are three distinct ways in which repression is channeled: (1) through the domestic banking system, (2) through savings accounts, and (3) through central banks. What these three "structural channels" have caused is that real interest rates (nominal interest rates adjusted for inflation) have become negative across many developed economies. This change in real interest rates has been helped by large demand for government debt from commercial banks and central banks. There is a risk premium associated with financial repression. For one, it presents a "demand premium" because without commercial and noncommercial players, interest rates might have been higher. To estimate "repression premium," Reinhart conducted empirical research on how long real interest rates remained negative as a result of policies seeking to repress government debt. In her research, she looked at a basic measure to identify periods of repression. This measure is the difference between short-term real interest rates, such as the Treasury bill adjusted for annual headline inflation, and real GDP. Whenever short-term real interest rates are consistently below real GDP, in combination with evidence of banks, individuals, and other institutions being required by regulation or other official incentive to hold government debt, there is a case of "financial repression." During such times, Reinhart found that inflation on average can run as high as 6 to 8 percent, while nominal government bond yields are about 2 to 4 percent below the inflation rate.

In her recent work titled "The Return of Financial Repression," Reinhart identified a new form of repression, namely the increased holdings of government bonds by central banks. According to estimates by the IMF economists Arslanalp and Tsuda in a study titled "Tracking Global Demand for Advanced Economy Sovereign

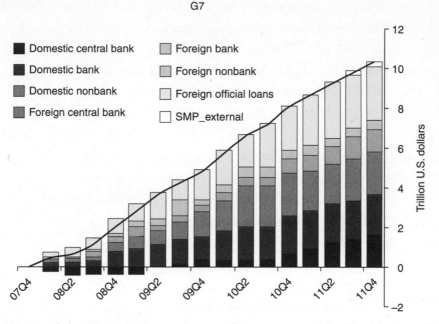

Figure 4.4 Cumulative purchases of government debt by the financial sector in G7.

(*Source:* Serkan Arslanalp and Takahiro Tsuda, "Tracking Global Demand for Advanced Economy Sovereign Debt," IMF Working Paper 284, 2012.)

Debt," domestic and foreign financial sectors of major industrialized countries ("G7") have cumulatively purchased $10 trillion in government bonds since 2004. That is about 15 percent of the outstanding government debt in the G7 countries. Of that $10 trillion amount, domestic central banks have purchased about $3.5 trillion as of the latest estimate in 2012, and their share is growing. Commercial banks, domestic and foreign, represent about another $3 to $4 trillion of debt holdings. The staggering trend of these purchases is displayed in Figure 4.4. A basic conclusion is that financial repression started perhaps earlier than the financial crisis, but the crisis has accelerated the trend.

Real interest rates in the G7 have all fallen since the early 2000s as a combination of the structural demand factor caused by financial repression along with expectations of lower growth going forward. Reinhart found that real interest rates in both advanced and emerging economies remained consistently lower than during the era of high capital mobility. The main reasons were binding interest rate ceilings on deposits that "induced" savers to purchase government bonds. Reinhart found there was a high frequency in distributions of real rates during the period of financial repression between 1945 and 1980. In the years that followed, high financial liberalization and entrepreneurship highlighted that lower real interest rates were universal. Since the 2008 crisis, real interest rates (measured by Treasury bills adjusted for inflation) have increasingly turned negative for the advanced economies. Reinhart's research distribution shows that negative real rates count for about half of the observations. These low to negative real interest rates are in contrast to risks of sovereign defaults in countries such as Argentina and Greece. So to measure the "financial repression premium," Figure 4.5 on page 111 shows the average real rates for the major advanced and emerging economies from 1945 to 2009. The legend in Figure 4.5 shows what the 3-year moving average is for real rates during repression, ranging from −1.9 to −4 percent. This same average has been in place since 2009 until today for G7 and several emerging countries. Negative real rates in emerging countries are often associated with artificially lower exchange rate values to keep competitiveness with other trading partners. And so risk-free rates are also much lower in real terms because of financial repression policies, presenting another embedded complexity. Moreover, financial repression "masks" the other risks identified, such as default and economic and political risk. Its subtlety creates an illusion that low risk-free rates are stable and safe, but in reality, they are being suppressed, and the investor earns a negative real return.

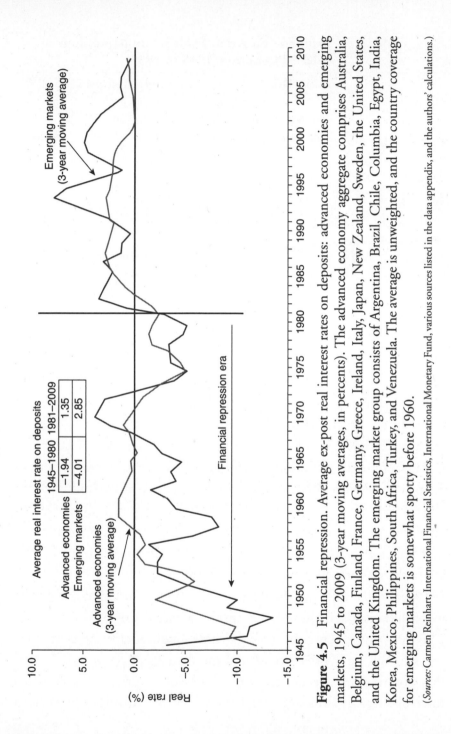

Figure 4.5 Financial repression. Average ex-post real interest rates on deposits: advanced economies and emerging markets, 1945 to 2009 (3-year moving averages, in percents). The advanced economy aggregate comprises Australia, Belgium, Canada, Finland, France, Germany, Greece, Ireland, Italy, Japan, New Zealand, Sweden, the United States, and the United Kingdom. The emerging market group consists of Argentina, Brazil, Chile, Columbia, Egypt, India, Korea, Mexico, Philippines, South Africa, Turkey, and Venezuela. The average is unweighted, and the country coverage for emerging markets is somewhat spotty before 1960.

(*Sources:* Carmen Reinhart, International Financial Statistics, International Monetary Fund, various sources listed in the data appendix, and the authors' calculations.)

Table 4.4   Reinhart's Empirical Evidence on Repression:
Selected Countries, 1945 to 1955

Country	Public Debt/GDP			Annual Average: 1946–1955	
	1945	1955 (Actual)	1955 Without Repression Savings (est.)	"Financial Repression Revenue"/GDP	Inflation
Australia	143.8	66.3	195.7	7.4	8.6
Belgium	112.6	63.3	130.1	5.7	3.4
Italy	66.9	38.1	120.2	13.3	9.6
Sweden	52.0	29.6	72.6	5.2	3.8
United Kingdom	215.6	138.2	233.8	2.6	3.9
United States	116.0	66.2	143.8	5.6	4.1

GDP, gross domestic product.
(*Source:* Carmen Reinhart, "The Return of Financial Repression," 2011.)

And so there have been 4 consecutive years of negative real short-term interest rates in major advanced economies since the financial crisis. In the definition of repression developed by Reinhart, negative real rates allow for stealth liquidation of government debt. The reason is that lower debt costs reduce debt service, which stops the growth of debt even when real GDP is near stall speed. Reinhart calls this the "liquidation effect," and Table 4.4 shows her empirical evidence. An important feature of repression is regulation that requires institutions and individuals to hold government debt. That pushes interest rates lower than what otherwise would have prevailed.

Reinhart found that liquidation of debt can occur during years when inflation surprises to the upside, a median of 5 to 6 percent. This happens when debt is significantly reduced (30 percent average fall) during a brief period of time (average, 1–3 years). Factors that connect debt reduction with higher or surprise inflation are a forceful austerity program or default and restructuring. A key reason is that large debt reduction allows for a quicker recovery in growth. Reinhart's evidence shows that real GDP growth rises on average by 2 percent in years after a big decline in outstanding gross government debt. Repression can also be subtle. In that case, regulatory rules can make people unaware or uncertain that they are being repressed. Reinhart's research has shown that when repression is subtle, it can take up to 20 years for debt to be reduced toward normal levels. During such a long period, real interest rates remain negative between 2 to 4 percent. Thus, the evidence on financial repression speaks. It has a close association with asset valuations through "portfolio balance." In that concept, there are two ways in which financial repression occurs. One is by committing to near zero interest rates for a very extended or unspecified time. That is a way in which central banks force negative real (and nominal) rates onto investors. Those investors feel "pressured" to seek alternative opportunities. Rather than exploring them in the real economy through tangible assets, they invest in other securities, such as corporate bonds. The other way is that central banks are nonsensitive price participants in the government bond market by purchasing large quantities. This activity depresses government bond yields but also creates the perception that government debt is underwritten by the central bank's balance sheet. This central bank commitment made the statement that government bonds are zero risk weighted even when their credit ratings are downgraded. With short-term interest rates near zero or negative, investors seek the yield curve for return. Ironically, this leads to allocating funds to government bonds despite paltry yield levels and higher risks. In the mind of investors, the price return from holding government bonds would be sufficient to offset the negative after tax real yield they earn. Not surprisingly, Treasuries, Gilts, Bunds, and JGBs have for that reason (among other reasons) remained in "demand."

There is another way in which repression prevails—the idea of "Tobin's Q," which is the ratio of enterprise market value to replacement cost. This ratio can be above 1, indicating that capital investment is attractive; a value below 1 says the opposite. Financial repression has an influence on market values because negative real rates lower the discount rates and thereby create higher net present values. Higher market values relative to fixed replacement cost should then increase investment. Conceptually, financial repression and Tobin's Q may have some merit. Tobin said: "The monetary authority forces market return on physical capital to diverge from its reproduction cost, thereby affecting rate of production and accumulation of capital assets." In essence, this has been driving central bank policy since 2008. Central banks cannot create economic outcomes directly by stating thresholds on unemployment or rejecting deflation. However, central banks can apply indirect ways of forcing financial asset returns onto capital. This process was going on since 2008 but with marginal success. During that time, the stock market was up 75 percent, but real GDP struggled at 2 percent. In the 1980s and 1990s, history has shown that such stock market performance would cause 4 to 5 percent real GDP growth. The Federal Reserve linking employment to Fed funds, the Bank of England moving to growth orientation, the Bank of Japan and the government taking initiative to end deflation, and the European Central Bank's focus on fragmentation are all examples of Tobin's Q idea. The main idea is to force negative real rates onto asset returns, which would eventually create an investment boom. The backdrop of heightened global uncertainty that did not seem to abate meant that to get capital spending and investment in a meaningful way, it would require equity and bond returns to go higher by lowering the real discount rates. That could have been accomplished only with more global financial repression via regulation (Basel III/Solvency II/Financial Services Authority), enthusiastic domestic audiences to hold government bonds, and central banks that remained actively engaged. As a result, the Folly of Financial Repression has driven real rates negative in many developed markets, potentially setting up a period of quicker debt reduction that would create room for higher inflation down the road.

The Liquidity Trap Premium

There has been an intense debate since the 1930s on whether an economy can fall into a "liquidity trap." Keynes identified a liquidity trap as a situation where interest rates are near zero but have no effect whatsoever. This happens when demand for money is perfectly inelastic, mostly because people save more out of uncertainty about the future. A liquidity trap can also exist when the money supply is perfectly inelastic. Low interest rates have no effect because of expectations that money supply creation would be fixed. The risk of such a trap may increase when a central bank decides to set a balance sheet target. Setting such a target in place for a period of time could have the same effect on expectations as setting the nominal policy rate near zero for an extended period of time. Although anchored policy rates can have a lower interest rate volatility and flatter yield curve effect, a balance sheet target could have a range bound effect on asset prices and risk premiums as the central bank provides a fixed rather than a variable level of liquidity. The longer the provided liquidity is fixed, the narrower risk premiums could get, specifically when the economy experiences disinflation that makes low nominal government bond yields still attractive in real terms. By keeping the balance sheet at a target level, the Federal Reserve may have created a liquidity trap, a fixed amount of liquidity that "traps" asset prices, referred to as the "asset price liquidity trap." Thus, a liquidity trap influenced by central bank money is a supply-driven liquidity trap. This is different from a demand-driven liquidity trap, which is traditionally known as the "Keynesian liquidity trap." According to the definition of the Keynesian liquidity trap, when bond yields reach a level at or close to the interest rate on the monetary base (interest on excess reserves), the demand for money can become infinitely inelastic. No matter how low interest rates are, the private sector's demand for money to invest and spend has become insensitive to the level of interest rates. In a supply-driven liquidity trap, money supply could become inelastic to interest rates when a substitution effect between risky and less risky assets disappears as future supplied central bank money is not fully replaced by the private sector. Fixing central bank liquidity effectively "traps" the private sector in bonds, and this effect is accentuated by the "preferred habitat" of investors that prefer a certain segment of the yield curve when it is steeply upward sloping.

Textbooks show that the money demand curve is downward sloping. When interest rates fall, demand for money should increase. The money supply curve is vertical when the supply of money is perfectly elastic at any level of interest rates. When demand for money becomes inelastic, the demand curve should be flat. When the money supply is inelastic, the supply curve could be horizontal. If the central bank keeps the money supply fixed by targeting a balance sheet size, and the money demand curve is assumed to be flat, then nominal rates may travel to a "new equilibrium." That would be where the flat money demand and horizontal money supply curves could meet. In Figure 4.6 on page 117, this idea is depicted by laying money demand and supply curves over the 5-year U.S. Treasury yield (x-axis) versus 2-year breakeven inflation from Treasury Inflation-Protected Securities (y-axis). The new equilibrium in the far left corner is where the asset price liquidity trap (inelastic money supply) meets the Keynesian liquidity trap (inelastic money demand). It is also conceivably the area where the central bank practices the most severe "confiscatory" policy by making the money supply inelastic, thereby forcing nominal rates excessively low. Unfortunately, this makes the liquidity trap worse, as asset prices are trapped in large sums of unproductive liquidity.

The analysis presents a dark picture. In an environment of macroeconomic volatility, keeping the central bank balance sheet size constant can create adverse liquidity conditions. This doesn't mean illiquidity. Rather, it implies "inelastic liquidity." This is liquidity that needs to be reinvested in instruments such as Treasury bills and short-term government bonds that offer no return whatsoever. This happens when financial repression is in effect via regulatory measures.

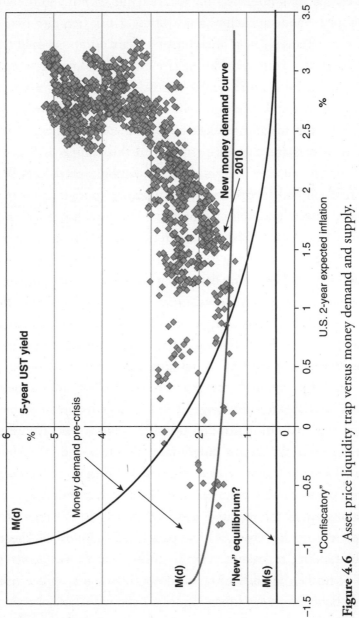

Figure 4.6 Asset price liquidity trap versus money demand and supply.

(*Source:* Bloomberg.)

A liquidity trap has been put into context with financial repression when a central bank influences the risk-free rate with liquidity. This has been dubbed "monetary repression." Thus, a risk-free rate under the influence of repression in a situation of a demand and supply type of liquidity trap may keep the risk-free rate excessively low for some time. The fact that there is no return to be made on the risk-free rate while inflation is higher and sovereign debt is not stable highlights how official influence can make the risk-free rate unnaturally riskier. The easiest way to understand the risk premium in this context is to compare short-term nominal rates with short-term inflation expectations. Because money demand and supply determine liquidity conditions in markets, short-term interest rates reflect expectations of liquidity. Such rates are overnight index swaps (OISs), a derivative of the central bank's overnight money market rate. Overnight index swaps are traded by banks and other parties in the over-the-counter derivatives market or exchange traded (for example, on the Chicago Mercantile Exchange) and quoted in both spot and forward terms. When comparing forward rates of overnight index swaps with short-term inflation expectations (e.g., measured by Treasury Inflation-Protected Securities), a liquidity trap premium can be "measured." The risk premiums here range from −1 to −2 percent for the major four economies (Figure 4.7 on page 119). The negative premium presents a negative expected real return that people have to accept. The reason is that the central banks keep overnight rates near zero, and so the forward rates on OISs are near zero, an expectation that return on cash remains nil for some time to come. Central bank policy geared at inducing inflation expectations causes this negative expected return. In the liquidity trap definition where risk aversion is high, people feel "comfortable" receiving a negative expected real return in the absence of alternatives, as well as the absence of further liquidity or credit creation that may entice risk taking. Until better economic times, Figure 4.7 shows that major economies suffer from a liquidity trap of some kind (supply or demand or both), as holding cash is induced by central banks as the viable alternative.

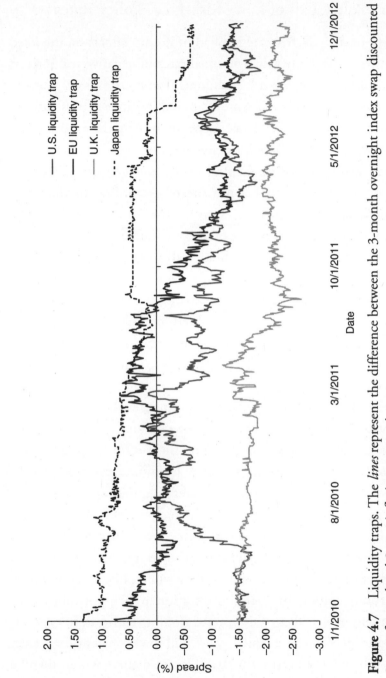

Figure 4.7 Liquidity traps. The *lines* represent the difference between the 3-month overnight index swap discounted 2 years forward and 2-year inflation expectations.

(*Source:* Bloomberg.)

Monetary Policy Exit of Low "Risk-Free" Policy Rates

The change of the risk-free rate has had profound effects on the fixed income universe. From negative nominal rates to negative real interest rates to historically narrow risk premiums, the presumption that the risk-free rate is no longer the same is something that carries further. The pension industry, for example, depends heavily on fixed income streams to match future liabilities, and low interest rates have challenged their business models. Central banks hold record amounts of government bonds on their balance sheets. According to the Bank for International Settlements, the sum is close to $3.5 trillion. The amount continues to grow because of ongoing quantitative easing programs. Such programs have a psychological incentive for investors to move further out on the risk spectrum. As a result, the central bank–stimulated investor demand led to the issuance in high-yield, corporate and covered bonds, as well as collateralized loan obligations reaching record highs in 2012. The changed risk-free rate altered demand for and supply of fixed income securities. As a result, interest rate expectations also changed.

There are a variety of theories that attempt to explain how expectations influence interest rates. The pure expectations hypothesis asserts that all government bonds have the same short-term expected return because investors with a risk-neutral view have the same kind of risk-seeking behavior. Thus, when interest rates rise, the capital losses for all bonds go up, and this would offset the higher yield advantage that bonds have relative to short-term, risk-free rates. In other words, if investors expect that their long-term bond investments will lose value because of an increase in interest rates, they will require a higher initial yield as a compensation for extending duration in their portfolios. This is a reason why the yield curve is upward sloping. Conversely, expectations of yield declines and capital gains will lower current long-term bond yields below the short-term rate. The yield curve would then be downward sloping or even inverted. This is how the yield curve would shift during past easing and tightening interest rate cycles. The slope of the yield curve provides a premium for inflation and liquidity. The slope was also a barometer of when the central bank might change policy. The financial crisis and the European debt crisis have changed that.

Other theories are put in question too, such as "market segmentation," which says that there is a preference for people to hold shorter- rather than longer-term bonds. In conjunction, "liquidity premium" says short-term bonds are desired, but longer-dated bonds get charged a liquidity premium. Central banks such as the Federal Reserve, Bank of England, European Central Bank, and Bank of Japan have all made direct or indirect commitments to keeping their benchmark policy rate near zero for an extended period of time. In the process, by accumulating government and other debt on their balance sheet, a risk transfer has taken place between the private and public sectors. This has implicitly changed the perception of the risk nature of the benchmark policy rate—that a central bank could infinitely expand its balance sheet and monetize potential losses or use accounting methods to amortize losses over time. The benchmark policy rate is riskier because of the central banks' diminished ability to raise interest rates in an effective manner. Given the large amounts of outstanding private and public debt, a sudden hike in interest rates may risk a disorderly deleveraging process. Federal Reserve Vice Chairman Janet Yellen has argued for an "optimal control" of the fed funds rate via enhanced communication strategies. In short, this innovative view of the policy rate is one that is "rules based" on economic targets or thresholds. Yellen dubbed it the "balanced approach" rule, how monetary policy guidance can adjust the fed funds rate expectations. She took the rule idea further by introducing the concept of optimal control—"a path is chosen to minimize the value of a specific 'loss function' conditional on a baseline forecast of economic conditions." As Figure 4.8 on page 122 shows, there are three paths by which the fed funds rate can adjust.

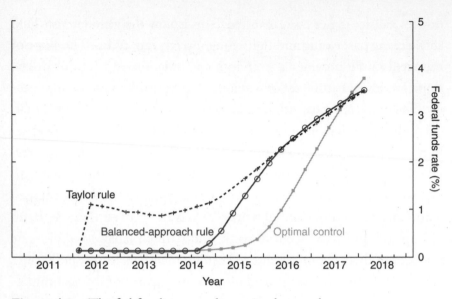

Figure 4.8   The fed funds rate under optimal control.
(*Source:* Federal Reserve.)

To change reservations toward risk taking, some academic proposals (e.g., from Columbia University) have suggested raising fed funds rate. A promise of low interest rates for an extended period could validate deflationary expectations that may perpetuate sluggish growth. By moving the Fed funds rate modestly higher, expectations of inflation could actually rise (if seen to be credible), and with that the nominal wage (over time). Another argument is that higher interest rates would stabilize the gap between investment and savings and change expectations of future returns. In a speech in late 2012, titled "The Economic Recovery and Economic Policy," Federal Reserve chairman Bernanke explained that U.S. unemployment was still about 2 to 2.5 percent above what would be a sustainable level (around 6 percent). At the same time, inflation as measured by the Personal Consumption Expenditures (PCE) index was below its target of 2 percent in 2012. In other words, the Federal Reserve has a dual mandate of fostering maximum employment and price stability. Given the nature of the sluggish U.S. economy at the time, the Federal Reserve saw its mandate as being out of balance. Within the Federal Open Market Committee (FOMC), support grew to use thresholds on both sides of its mandate to steer the fed funds rate higher. A variety of Fed officials as well as Bernanke said that an allowable deviation from the inflation target could be "a few tenths." Thus, a threshold for the FOMC to take action would be if inflation is above 2.5 percent *and* if unemployment is closer to 6.5 percent. A liftoff in the fed funds rate would be possible if both sides of the mandate were in balance. The two "thresholds" are depicted in Figure 4.9 on page 124 as *dotted lines* versus the unemployment rate, PCE index, and the fed funds rate. The graph suggests two things. With the PCE threshold having room for about 0.6 percent versus the 2 percent target, inflation expectations could go much higher. In the same speech, Bernanke stated that because the 2008 crisis aftermath had had such an effect on output, potential GDP had possibly fallen below 2 percent. The fed funds rate has historically been correlated with nominal GDP and thereby potential GDP. When it would be time for the fed funds rate to rise, a neutral, fair level could also be more like 2 percent. Coming from a level at the zero bound for a number of years, this could mean a significant adjustment in not only short-term but also longer-term interest rates.

And so the threshold policy of the Federal Reserve became reality. On December 12, 2012, the Federal Reserve released the following statement:

> In particular, the Committee decided to keep the target range for the federal funds rate at 0 to 1/4 percent and currently anticipates that this exceptionally low range for the federal funds rate will be appropriate at least as long as the unemployment rate remains above 6-1/2 percent, inflation between one and two years ahead is projected to be no more than a half percentage point above the Committee's 2 percent longer-run goal.

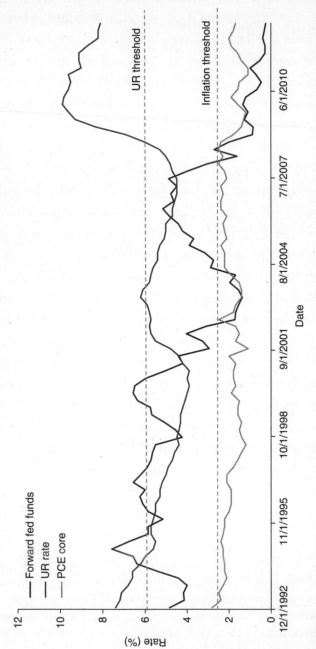

Figure 4.9 The U.S. fed funds rate and thresholds for it to change. Personal Consumption Expenditures (PCE); unemployment rate (UR).

(*Source*: Bloomberg, quarterly data series, 1992–2012.)

This introduced a brand new way of conducting monetary policy, particularly how Federal Reserve policy would become much more dependent on economic variables than before.

Moreover, the idea was to keep interest rates at historically low levels for probably the next 10 years. This has changed expectations about how and when the fed funds rate would adjust in the future. As Figure 4.10 on page 126 shows, as of late 2012, the expectations were that the Federal Reserve would very gradually raise interest rates to a terminal rate of 2 percent in 2022. The timing of that exit of loose monetary policy and ultra-low interest rates may have an agenda attached. When Federal Reserve chairman Bernanke and Bank of England governor King's terms expire in 2013 and 2014, they will leave legacies of the most extraordinary monetary policy actions in history. Their legacies are tainted, as such policies did not produce meaningful economic results. With both the U.S. and the U.K. governments putting off achieving near-term budget deficit targets, monetary policy took the lead to drive economies. Bernanke and King's legacies not being followed through by their successors could be one way in which unconventional policy will eventually be exited. As much as unconventional policy was deeply entrenched within the Federal Reserve and the Bank of England, an incoming chairman and governor might have different ideas. Slowly but surely, unconventional policy would end as the new chairman and governor would advocate change. The other way is "practical limits." For example, those limits are negative rates having a distorting effect on market functioning. The technical nature of these limits has, to an extent, blocked transmission channels over the past few years. As those limits become overpowering, the effectiveness of monetary policy could be further reduced.

Government debt also plays an important role. The European Central Bank's role in the Greek debt crisis remains the precedent for how monetary policy has to act as a "special creditor" in sovereign restructurings. If the ECB had decided to take a haircut (loss) on its Greek bond holdings during Greek debt restructuring in 2012, it would have allowed for significant monetary easing in Greece, as such

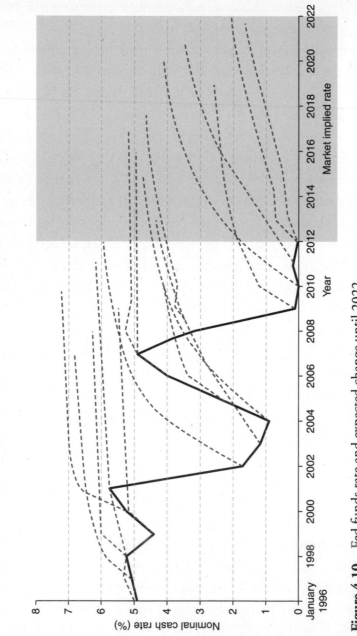

Figure 4.10 Fed funds rate and expected change until 2022.

(*Source:* Bloomberg, Grantham Mayo van Otterloo [GMO] LLC.)

a haircut would have provided debt relief. The ECB refused to do that in the interest of taxpayers' money, including that of the taxpayers in Greece. The taxpayers never benefited from the ECB bond holdings, however. In fact, the taxpayers in northern Europe had to pay for the bailouts of Greece, Ireland, Portugal, Spain, and Cyprus. The taxpayers in those countries didn't benefit either, as the bailout funds were partially used to redeem Greek government debt held on the ECB balance sheet.

The "stock effect" of central bank holdings may see statutory limits at some point through the political process. The limit is intended to keep monetary policy independent, specifically when the debt stock as a percent of GDP held on the central bank's balance sheet is too large to be redeemed by the national Treasury. It has become increasingly problematic for major central banks to maintain independence. As the balance sheet grew and the Treasury owed more debt to the Federal Reserve, the fed funds rate and Treasury bill rates resemble essentially the same rate. Given the amount of outstanding federal debt and unfunded liabilities, the fed funds rate is then no longer the ultimate risk-free rate.

Long-Term Real Rates Expectations

In a paper titled "Monetary Policy and Long Term Real Rates," FOMC member Jeremy Stein and Federal Reserve staff economist Samuel G. Hanson tested how monetary policy affects forward real rates. As a rule of thumb, Stein and Hanson find that every 1 percent increase in 2-year nominal yields on the day the Fed makes a decision is associated with a 0.5 percent rise in the 10-year forward real rate. Forward real rates can be dissected into expected real rates and real term premium. Expected real rates are what markets discount to be the yield on a bond adjusted for future inflation. The term "premium" is the difference between short- and long-term interest rates, as explained in the slope of the yield curve. Stein and Hanson argue that the main channel to stimulate the economy would be to lower the term premium. The focus is on "yield orientation," whereby a fall in short-term rates leads to a rebalancing of a portfolio toward longer bonds to keep the overall portfolio yield level the same. This is a "pure" term premium effect, driven by supply and demand for term premium rather than changes in short-term interest rate expectations. In their test of a basic supply and demand model, Stein and Hanson analyze two types of investors: "expected return–oriented" investors who buy longer-maturity bonds and finance them with short-term funds, and the "yield-oriented" investors who yield income from holding long bonds instead of short-maturity bonds. This model shows that yield-oriented investors in particular bring down term premiums irrespective of the days when the Fed makes decisions. The evidence is that publicly traded commercial banks are yield oriented and use a steep yield curve for accounting, regulatory capital, and reported earnings purposes. Stein concludes that the term premium–seeking investors in the government bond market may see a spillover to the credit markets. Some other Fed researchers have found a relationship through increased corporate issuance when short-term interest rates fall or are kept low by a central bank.

Taking all of this together, the risk-free rate at zero embeds a significant risk of an upward adjustment of the fed funds rate and benchmark policy rates in major advanced economies at some point in the future. The timing thereof remains speculative and highly dependent on the global economic outlook. It means that whether one is a yield- or expected return–oriented investor, the income stream on bonds derived from the slope of the yield curve may change in the future.

How to Look at Risk Premiums

If the risk-free interest rate has changed in terms of risk profile even if its absolute level does not reflect this yet, what would this imply for risk premiums in general? A premium over a comparable Treasury bill or government bond is a compensation for additional risk that the investor is taking. When risk premiums are narrow, the compensation is seen as inadequate, and vice versa. Market participants, academics, and policymakers often have lengthy discussions about what the "fair" level of risk premiums should be. To justify a risk premium, two components are important: (1) the return or yield of the riskier asset and (2) the level of the risk-free rate itself. The discussions in this chapter have centered on the components under (2). When these are compared with the risk components under (1), it cannot be automatically argued that each cancels out the other. For stocks, the risk premium is the expected return on equity, which is the sum of the dividend yield and capital gains, minus the risk-free rate. The risk premium for equities is also called the "equity risk premium."

In the context of bonds, the term "risk premium" is often used imprecisely to refer to credit spread (i.e., the difference between the bond interest rate and the risk-free rate). To see why this is inconsistent with the given definition, imagine that the risk-free rate is 2 percent and corporate bonds are yielding 6 percent. Does that mean that the expected return in excess of the risk-free rate is 4 percent? Almost certainly not; after all, there is surely a positive probability of a default, as well as a positive probability of positive or negative capital gains caused by fluctuations in the market prices of bonds. In reality, the risk premium is likely to be significantly less than the credit spread; it could even be negative if the bond's default scenarios are negatively correlated with most other bonds' default scenarios. And for an asset to be risk free, its actual return should (in theory) match the expected return. The reality is that markets never assign 100 percent probability to that being the case, justifying the existence of risk premiums. There is also reinvestment risk. This risk occurs when there is a shift in the yield curve due to a change in expectations of inflation and growth. As these expectations are dynamic, the likelihood of reinvesting a matured bond at the exact same interest rate is quite low. Thus, one has to derive two types of risk premiums to assess the impact of a change in the risk-free rate and what it may mean for other financial assets. The first one, as mentioned, is the equity risk premium; the second is the bond risk premium. The bond risk premium has been estimated by, for example, John Cochrane of the National Bureau of Economic Research as the sum of expected returns of bonds across the yield curve. This sum would be the level of interest rates, the slope of the yield curve, and the curvature that measures the change in the yield curve slope. Cochrane found a strong correlation between expected returns and forward rates, as well as between forward rates and macroeconomic variables. On that basis, a bond's forward yield relative to a short-term interest rate can be an "approximation" of the bond risk premium.

When comparing the bond risk premium with the equity risk premium, there is a distinct relationship. As depicted in Figure 4.11 on page 131, the "adjusted" bond and equity risk premium trend with each other. The adjusted premium is calculated by adding default risk and reinvestment risk to a 5-year Treasury yield 5 years forward and a 3-month Treasury bill. The default risk can be measured by CDS spread/ (1 − recovery ratio). Reinvestment risk assumes that expected return (measured by the forward yield) does not equal actual return (the current yield on a bond). The trend in Figure 4.11 shows the inverse relationship in the 1990s when U.S. government debt default risk was considered "nil" and when the interest rate cycle was "normal." This means that interest rates were tightened or loosened by the Federal Reserve as growth and inflation changed. By the early 2000s, this had changed when the risk of deflation in 2003 changed the perception of Fed tightening cycles going forward. In addition, the sovereign CDS market became more tradable as of 2005, which allowed market participants to judge the implied default probabilities on government debt. Since the 2008 crisis, when the Fed funds reached a lower zero bound, bond and equity risk premiums were on the rise until they were in close

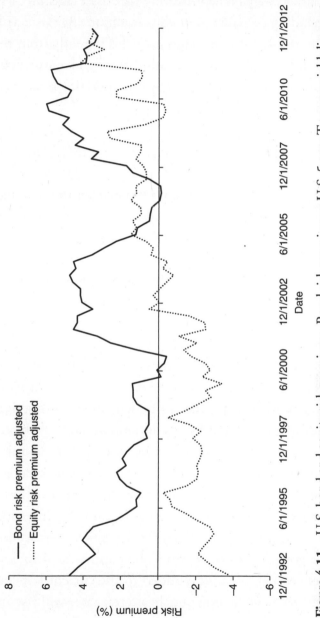

Figure 4.11 U.S. bond and equity risk premiums. Bond risk premium = U.S. 5-year Treasury yield discount 5 years forward − U.S. 3-month Treasury bill. Equity risk premium = 1/price-earnings ratio S&P index − U.S. 5-year Treasury yield discounted 5 years forward.

(*Source:* Bloomberg, quarterly data series, 1992–2012.)

proximity (about 4 percent) to each other by the end of 2012. This suggests that markets were perhaps treating each asset class with a similar risk by demanding the same premium. Additionally, this may have implied that the risk-free rate is being judged differently from before the 2008 crisis. It has created the realization among investors that risk premiums have to be judged differently by incorporating more risk elements embedded in the risk-free rate.

Conclusion

This chapter has attempted in a basic way to explain the "complexity premium" of the risk-free rate. The embedded premium does not exist just through liquidity with no or limited default risk. The amount of additional premium shows that the current risk-free rates are well below where they could be. Analyzing the different components of risk factors, it would be rather simple just to add them together to the existing level of the risk-free rate. However, the different premiums characterize the angles of what the true risk-free rate could look like.

In an investment management framework, it is important to understand what the risk-free rate does for a portfolio. At its core, it functions as a rate at which cash can be reinvested. It functions as a discount rate for government bonds and a base rate to which risk premiums are added to value agency, covered, corporate, municipal, high-yield, and mortgage bonds. The risk-free rate plugs into equity valuations, too, as well as pricing of derivatives such as options, futures, and swaps. It would be too simple to sum the different risk premiums and determine what would be the new risk-free rate for everything else going forward. It would be controversial to suggest that the sum of the risk premiums added to the current level of the risk-free rate suggests that is how much interest rates will rise in the future. The "new" risk-free rate does not necessarily suggest a fair level of short-term interest rates.

The dynamics of economic growth itself much more determine what potentially the ultimate destination of a risk-free rate could be. Growth is what matters in a time of overindebtedness. As Benjamin Graham argued in his *Security Analysis* work of 1934: "GDP is ultimately the source of all cash flows and returns that trickle down into various financial assets based on their individual seniority and place in the economic capital structure." This means that GDP determines the level of returns and bond yields as well as the size of risk premiums. Thus, the risk premium analysis in this chapter may provide a good indication of where the total sum of risk premiums is high or low so that an investor can use that information for relative value between fixed income and equity asset classes. Therefore, if a country has a very high risk premium, it could mean that a portfolio should shift entirely to other types of fixed income securities or stocks than being invested in government bonds. The opposite may be assumed when risk premiums are very low.

Most of the major economies are somewhere in the middle. Their interest rates are low, but so is the risk of default, and there is even less evidence of repression or a liquidity trap. There is a case to be made that a portfolio should be a broad set of stocks and bonds, perhaps what one traditionally is accustomed to. The portfolio has to seek "alternatives" to the risk-free rate, as further discussed in Chapter 5.

Chapter 5

Where and What to Invest In:
The "Alternatives"

A shrinking universe of AAA-rated government bonds has presented alternatives. Figure 5.1 on page 136, taken from the International Monetary Fund (IMF) 2012 stability report, shows what other potentially "safe" securities exist. The universe is substantial, estimated at $74.4 trillion, of which AAA-/AA-rated government bonds represent the majority ($33 trillion). Some of the asset classes, such as agency bonds, supranational debt, and covered bonds, have low risk premiums relative to U.S. Treasuries. They are increasingly taking over the role of government bonds as traditional collateral, liquidity instrument, and benchmark rate to value other assets. In the following subsections, several of these asset classes are discussed to evaluate them as "alternative risk-free rate" investments with the emphasis being that these investments are *not* risk free, as the analysis will show.

What to Invest In: Covered Bonds

Before the onset of the credit crisis in 2008, covered bonds were generally seen by investors as a generic triple-A-quality asset class.

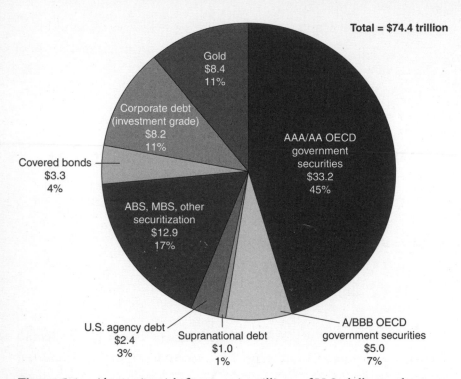

Figure 5.1   Alternative risk-free rates in trillions of U.S. dollars and percent of total. Data for government and corporate debt are as of 2011, quarter 2; supranational debt, covered bonds, and gold as of the end of 2012; and U.S. agency debt and securitization as of 2011, quarter 3. ABS, asset-backed securities; MBS, mortgage-backed securities; OECD, Organisation for Economic Co-operation and Development.

(*Source:* International Monetary Fund Financial Stability Report, 2012.)

Valuations were homogeneous across all jurisdictions and reflected assumptions of near zero default probability and negligible loss severities because of their long history since their advent in 1769. Covered bonds are securities issued by a financial institution and backed by a group of loans residing on the balance sheet known as the "cover pool." The assets in the pools can consist of high-quality private mortgage loans, public sector loans, or a mix of the two. Central to the success of the asset class—and correspondingly, its valuations—is the dual recourse characteristic. This means that covered bond investors are given a priority claim to a segregated on-balance sheet pool of assets parallel with a senior claim on the issuer. The claim ranks the covered bondholders pari passu with senior unsecured creditors. Traditional covered bond investors showed high confidence in the asset class by requiring a low risk premium to "risk-free" assets such as U.S. Treasuries. In hindsight, this view of covered bonds could be seen as noncommensurate with the actual credit, refinancing, and liquidity risks inherent in covered bonds.

These risks have revealed themselves in recent episodes of market stress from 2008 to 2012 as the credit strength of issuing entities and the quality of cover pool collateral were questioned. During the financial crisis, the credit strength of the financial credit sector as a whole came under scrutiny. As is commonly known, central to the problem was nonperformance of mortgage assets resulting from loose origination standards, complex securitization techniques, and deteriorating underlying macroeconomic variables such as declining house prices and rising unemployment. More recently, the credit risk of public sector loans from distressed European economies experienced a similar reassessment in 2010 to 2012. The natural consequence of weakening collateral performance and issuer credit fundamentals has been the scrutiny of structural features of individual covered bond programs. Although simplistic compared with asset-backed securities (ABSs) or mortgage-backed securities (MBSs) because covered bond structures are on balance sheets and do not use securitization techniques such as "tranching" or subordination, covered pools are dynamic open structures. The issuer may add and remove cover pool assets (i.e., mortgage or public sector loans) or issue or retire liabilities (covered bonds). Thus, the cover pool is "live" and is continuously mutating. Credit enhancement features, asset liability amortization mismatches, and collateral performance thus change with time. Consequently, a concern associated with covered bonds is less than perfect transparency. However, the market is expanding rapidly, in terms of both secondary market liquidity and primary market supply. This growth has been fueled by three main factors:

1. Strong demand from a large investor base of natural buyers
2. Regulatory developments such as Basel III and Solvency II
3. Explicit support from central banks like the European Central Bank (ECB) via its Covered Bond Purchase Programme (ended late 2012)

This combination has created a vibrant environment and global momentum for covered bonds. The U.S. covered bond market has seen a revival since 2010, when foreign issuers opportunistically entered the market. Since then, approximately $105 billion has been issued as of December 2012, according to data compiled by Barclays and Bank of America, and more foreign issuers are seeking to tap the U.S. investor base. But the U.S. issuer covered bond market itself is almost nonexistent, with just a few legacy covered bonds outstanding that were issued during the financial crisis. In November 2011, the U.S. Covered Bond Act was introduced in the U.S. Senate by Senators Kay Hagen (D-NC) and Bob Corker (R-TN), and co-sponsored by Chuck Schumer (D-NY). The bill expands on the bill introduced in the House in April 2011, but some of the outstanding issues remain unresolved. These are the Federal Deposit Insurance Corporation's (FDIC's) concern about covered bondholders' seniority over depositors, the eligible collateral appropriate for covered pools, and the extent of overcollateralization permitted. Overcollateralization means amassing more collateral than is necessary to obtain financing, which is sometimes used to improve credit ratings. If the bill finds bipartisan support in both the House and the Senate, it may pass sometime in 2013 or 2014. And if so, then under the current 4 percent bank liability limit introduced by the FDIC in 2008, the U.S. domestic covered bond market could reach $500 billion over the next 3 to 5 years, according to a Deutsche Bank research report dated January 10, 2012.

The biggest foreign issuers in the U.S. covered bond market are the major Canadian banks. The banks issued covered bonds against loans in a pool that were originated under Canadian Mortgage Housing Corporation (CMHC) programs. These programs had an explicit backing from the Canadian government on mortgage insurance. This explicit backing is somewhat similar to what the United States has in place with Fannie Mae or Freddie Mac in conservatorship. Because of the overheating of the Canadian housing market, the Canadian government decided to implement legislation that limited CMHC insurance on mortgage loans. That capped the total amount of mortgage origination under the CMHC program at $600bn across the Canadian banks. The existing Canadian covered bonds were issued under the CMHC program with insured mortgage loans in the covered pool. That mortgage insurance is backed by the full faith and credit of the Canadian government. When the change in legislation was passed in the Canadian parliament, the outstanding Canadian covered bonds were grandfathered because the loans in the covered pool did not lose their Canadian government guarantee on insurance. One of the Canadian banks, Royal Bank of Canada (RBC), filed a registered shelf with the Securities and Exchange Commission to issue covered bonds in the United States. This would allow the RBC to access the U.S. retail market. The success of the RBC's program was underpinned by the CMHC, which designed a "Canadian Registered Covered Bond Program." The program outlined the collateral specifics and other requirements under which Canadian banks can issue covered bonds in Canada and elsewhere. The program, which offers greater transparency in pool collateral, attracted investors. To date, Canadian covered bonds represent the largest share of the U.S. covered bond market.

Covered Bonds Going Global

Globally, the covered bond market stands at approximately $3.3 trillion, according to the IMF. While these were traditionally issued mostly in Europe, more countries have recently joined the covered bond market by enacting a legal framework. Iceland, Russia, Romania, India, South Korea, Chile, the United States, Japan, Singapore, Malaysia, Indonesia, and even China are examples of new frontier markets in covered bonds (Figure 5.2).

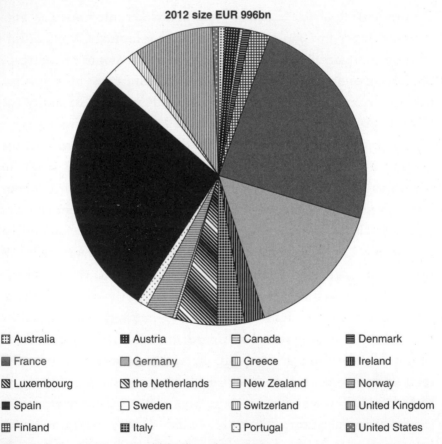

Figure 5.2   Main covered bond markets. 2012.

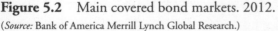

(*Source:* Bank of America Merrill Lynch Global Research.)

The globalization of the covered bond market is forecasted to gather pace in 2013 to 2014. The trend, which has seen supply in the euro market shrink from EUR195bn in 2011 to EUR100bn in 2012, was expected to continue as non-European jurisdictions open up and banks seek to diversify their funding. According to Barclays, 2012 was the first time that global covered bond issuance from non-euro area countries exceeded issuance from euro area countries. A combination of bank deleveraging, improved access to unsecured funding, and banks' desire to preserve assets for funding from the ECB is driving the decline in issuance by European banks. The U.S. dollar market and other currencies—such as Australian and Canadian dollars and Swiss francs—could increase by almost 50 percent in 2013, according to Barclays research. Covered bond volumes in many other markets may also be boosted by the new legal frameworks that are being introduced, including those in South Korea, Panama, Mexico, Morocco, New Zealand, Singapore, and possibly the United States.

But for European banks, many question marks remain. Banks' reliance on central banks for funding is expected to continue. Retained covered bonds for ECB repurchase financing ("repo") purposes, which reached a record 306 billion euros—primarily out of Spain, France, and Italy, according to data from Barclays for the 12-month period ending in October 2012—were expected to remain a theme. Thus, benchmark covered bond issuance from euro area credit institutions may be restricted to optimize funding. New jurisdictions such as Belgium are expected to make the most of their newly set-up frameworks, and issuance from non-European banks will help keep the euro market alive. Although covered bonds continue to be considered a "safe-haven" funding tool for issuers as well as a relatively secure place for investors to invest, some trouble spots should be noted. According to rating agency Moody's, ongoing negative pressure on sovereigns and issuers could continue to threaten issuer and covered bond credit quality in the future. European covered bond downgrades increased sharply in 2012, when the amount of downgrades was twice as high as the level seen in the previous 4 years. In relation to bail-ins, although secured liabilities are on the face of it excluded from the scope of the bail-in tool, there is room under the terms of the European Commission's Crisis Management Directive to allow for a potential carve-out if secured liabilities exceed the value of the assets securing them.

In June 2012, the European Commission said that member states were allowed to exempt covered bonds from the provision. This could lead to uncertainty for the asset class because it will come down to the value individual national regulators may attach to covered bonds. From an investor's perspective, this may add an element of uncertainty to the analysis of the risk factors involved in covered bonds. Another caveat for covered bonds has been the liquidity factor. During the 2008 financial crisis, covered bonds suffered large losses because banks were unwilling to make sufficient markets and provide liquidity outside of the government bond markets. In an extensive analysis, the Bank for International Settlements (BIS) looked at the liquidity difference between covered bonds and government bonds during and after the crisis. Figure 5.3 on page 143 shows the historical liquidity risk.

The BIS found that before and after the crisis, government bonds were slightly more liquid than covered bonds in both the short- and long-term market segments. During the 2008 crisis, liquidity decreased in both markets, but the covered bond market was less liquid than the government bond market for any trade size. The BIS's second finding was that the price impact of a trade was lower in interdealer markets than in dealer–client markets. After the 2008 crisis, the liquidity risk decreased to the pre-crisis levels. The exception was in the market for long-term covered bonds, where liquidity risk remained somewhat higher. An associated risk is when longer-dated covered bondholders are "time subordinated." That means that shorter-maturity covered bonds are repaid ahead of longer-maturity covered bonds in case of an issuer default or liquidation.

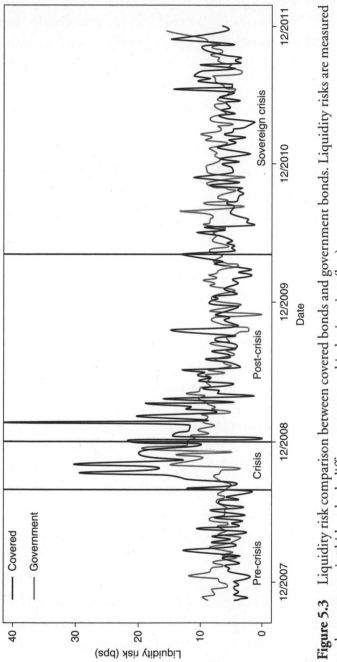

Figure 5.3 Liquidity risk comparison between covered bonds and government bonds. Liquidity risks are measured as the average price bid and ask difference measured in basis points (bps).

(*Source:* International Monetary Fund.)

In a report released in May 2010, Moody's warned that when an issuer defaults, "later-maturing covered bonds are subject to time subordination." Moody's judged that principal cash collections are used on a first-come, first-served basis, paying earlier-maturing covered bonds before later-maturing ones. If so, this may lead to erosion of overcollateralization of the underlying covered pool. This may worsen the credit rating of a covered pool and thereby the rating of covered bonds. There is also asset–liability risk. Covered bonds are repaid independent of the cash flows of the covered pool. Likewise, the cash flows received from the total assets become part of the regular cash flows from the covered pool. This could imply an asset–liability mismatch underlying a covered bond. If this asset–liability mismatch was completely uncontrolled, then the obligation to repay covered bonds would have been no different from an obligation to repay any secured or unsecured bond issued by the originator. Hence, the strength of a covered bond depends on how wide the asset–liability mismatch is. If the asset–liability mismatch is too wide, a covered bond leans too heavily on the liquidity strengths of the issuer and therefore is no different from a corporate bond. If the asset–liability mismatch is negligible, a covered bond leans toward being more like an MBS.

Covered Bond Valuation

Covered bonds being seen increasingly as a surrogate for sovereign bonds have made the asset class a focal point of attention in portfolio selection. This has brought forward a discussion of how to value covered bonds. Traditional credit investors deciding whether to invest in covered bonds typically investigate movement in the yield difference versus senior unsecured corporate bonds such as those issued by banks. The yield difference presents a trade-off for an investor. When the difference is narrow, it indicates that the risk assigned to a senior unsecured bond is viewed to be too low. The reason is that a senior unsecured bond has a claim on assets that is different from that of a covered bond. In addition, the covered bond has dual recourse on both the assets in the covered pool and those of the company. Thus, when the yield difference between senior unsecured and covered bonds is small, it indicates that there is a mismatch in risk assignment of assets. This can blur to an extent the relative value consideration of each asset class. Investors should also consider details on pool (over) collateralization and the possibility of recourse to the sponsor bank (issuer) in case of residual covered claims above and beyond the covered pool. In case of the latter, recourse could be junior or on a pari-passu basis with the senior unsecured debt holders. This means that investment decisions between covered bonds and senior unsecured debt can result from relative value views on the difference between corporate recovery rates and recovery on covered pool collateral.

In practice, pool recovery estimates are based on historical performance of similar mortgage loans without adjusting for forward-looking economic scenarios. Forward-looking scenario analysis is made more complicated, in part, by the revolving nature of the collateral pool and the lack of transparency on the underlying loan characteristics. When considering investment decisions, nominal yield spread analysis may become insufficient because investors must now consider recovery and default risk under various economic conditions. To calculate relative value or break-even analysis, a factor-based approach could be used. The attractiveness of this approach is that it provides a means to quantify default probabilities across a range of outcomes. In the MBS market, there are what's called "one-factor models." These have a single variable, namely home price appreciation (HPA). A borrower's credit risk, as measured by a range of scores and levels of financial documentation, is an important underwriting criterion. However, as ample empirical evidence over the past decade has shown, the mortgagor's default incentive remains directly tied to the amount of negative home equity. By extension, the covered bond issuer's default probability is also impacted by home price depreciation (1) via direct primary impacts on bank portfolio retained loans and MBS and (2) through secondary effects because housing is strongly correlated with consumer and corporate credit held on banks' balance sheets.

On the flip side to benefits, the fact remains that models are by definition simplified versions of complex financial mechanisms. As such, they are susceptible to biases or sensitivities that possibly could lead to an incorrect relative value view. Thus, Figure 5.4 shows loss-adjusted yields (reflecting the possibility of default and recovery) under a range of HPA scenarios for a representative covered bond. This covered bond is backed by a collateral pool of pay-option adjustable-rate mortgage (ARM) loans originated in 2006. (Pay-option ARMs allow borrowers to choose from a number of different payment options each month.) The chart also shows the loss-adjusted yield for a representative senior prime pass-through (SR FLT PT) security backed by floating rate

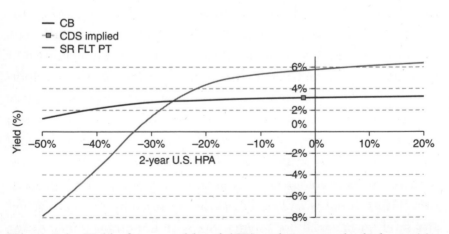

Figure 5.4 Yield of a covered bond (CB) and mortgage-backed securities (representative senior prime pass-through [SR FLT PT]) under different house price scenarios.

(*Sources:* Moody's, Pacific Investment Management Company [PIMCO], and Bloomberg.)

collateral originated in the same year. When using mortgage prepayment models, the covered bond nominal yield without credit default possibility is 3.31 percent. The yield, however, declines to 3.12 percent (a reduction of 19 basis points) when calculating returns on a loss-adjusted basis by incorporating credit default swap (CDS) implied default likelihood and estimated recovery from the covered bond collateral pool. The SR FLT PT, in comparison, returns significantly higher yields in base and modest stress scenarios, yet returns negative yields in the case of severe economic HPA shock, as shown on the left side of the chart.

Investors in residential mortgage-backed securities (RMBSs) typically demand a higher return over other securities because of embedded optionality (of mortgage prepayment and default) that results in cash flow uncertainty and that does not exist—or exists to a much lesser extent—in other securities such as the covered bond. The break-even point, or a macroeconomic economic shock in which hypothetical RMBS and covered bond returns are equal, in this example is −27 percent 2-year U.S. housing price appreciation. This implies that for investors who can tolerate some risk of losing a significant portion of principal, if their view is one of dire economic outlook, the higher-returning asset would be the covered bond. That said, different assumptions will lead to different results. This relative value analysis would potentially be more accurate if the exact loan level details on the covered pool were known instead of estimating collateral performance from general pool-level characteristics. This example demonstrates that valuation of a covered bond when using sophisticated mortgage prepayment technology shows that the covered bond has a "steady" return profile under different stress scenarios. That is, a covered bond does have credit risk, liquidity risk, and default risk. A covered bond is therefore not risk free, and its annual return profile has at times shown high variance. Investing in covered bonds requires bottom-up analysis by looking at comparable MBS securities from the same issuer and regularly published covered pool data. Covered bonds are not government bonds or agency bonds; rather they are credits. They can be an addition to a portfolio in terms of diversifying exposure to senior unsecured or corporate bonds, especially when they are shared by the same issuer.

What to Invest In: Corporate Bonds

Corporate bonds have been traditionally issued by Fortune 500 companies, but also by smaller businesses. Corporate bonds have been around since 1860, have taxable (state and federal) coupon interest, have typically an investment grade credit rating, and are subject to default risk. They have grown in popularity over the past two decades, with an even bigger investment audience since the 2008 crisis. As a result, issuance of corporate bonds rose, and inflows into funds that specialize in that sector reached new records in 2012. Corporate bond sales from the United States to Europe and Asia surpassed 2009's record to reach $3.89 trillion in 2012 as borrowing costs plunged to historically low levels. The Barclays Global Aggregate Credit Index yield reached a low of 2.56 percent by late 2012. Global issuance of corporate bonds was up to $3.29 trillion in 2012 versus $3.23 trillion in 2010, and investors funneled an unprecedented $455.7 billion into corporate bond funds in 2012, according to Bloomberg data. The extra yield that investors demand to own corporate bonds rather than government debt was on average 223 basis points (2.3 percent) by the end of 2012, narrowing from 351 basis points at the end of 2011, according to Bank of America Merrill Lynch research. Corporate borrowing costs have tumbled from an all-time high of 9.05 percent in October 2008 after the collapse of Lehman Brothers. Despite these staggering numbers, at the end of 2012, the projected issuance of corporate bonds was set to fall in 2013, with "net issuance" (different between gross issuance and coupon payments or redemptions) trending lower. This is shown

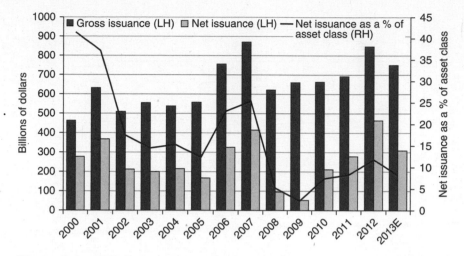

Figure 5.5 U.S. investment grade gross and net issuance. LH, left-hand scale; RH, right-hand scale. Annual data for 2000 to 2013.
(*Source:* J.P. Morgan.)

in Figure 5.5. It is noteworthy that gross issuance in 2012 reached the pre-crisis peak but with ever so much more demand from pension funds and money managers.

Historically, corporate bonds have always yielded higher than U.S. Treasuries. There are also high-yield corporate bonds that have a lower than investment grade rating. The yields of these securities are traditionally higher than those of investment-grade corporate bonds. In Figure 5.6 on page 150, the yields are shown of the Barclays U.S. Aggregate Bond Index (investment grade) and the Barclays U.S. Corporate High Yield Index, both plotted against the 10-year Treasury yield. This simple picture shows how the yields have closely correlated at times, but then show a sharp divergence during recessions, such as during 1991, 2001, and 2008. Since 2009, however, the trend correlation seems to have intensified.

One explanation has been that quantitative easing by the Federal Reserve encouraged investors to rotate out of Treasuries into riskier

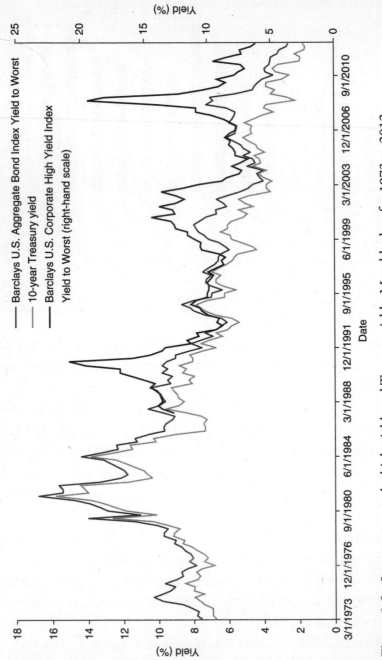

Figure 5.6 Investment-grade, high-yield, and Treasury yields. Monthly data for 1973 to 2012.
(*Sources*: Bloomberg and Barclays.)

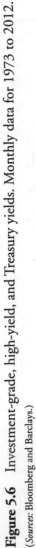

assets such as corporate bonds. Two other plausible reasons are that corporations have "healthy balance sheets" with large cash balances, which has attracted investors to their bonds. Another reason, as shown in Figure 5.5, is that net issuance of corporate bonds has been falling steadily as companies mostly refinanced their existing debt stock. This has created a further fall in corporate bond yields to near record lows. Figure 5.6 may suggest that corporate bonds have been sought out as an alternative to U.S. Treasuries, but by no means are corporate bonds "risk free." In fact, the sharp spikes in corporate bond yields during 1988 to 1991, 2001 to 2002, and 2008 to 2009 were accompanied by a rise in average default rates to high single digits, according to Moody's research. Thus, when investing in corporate bonds, the risk premium, being the difference between the yield of a corporate and Treasury bond yield, embeds a variety of credit and liquidity risks. Darrell Duffee showed empirical evidence of a negative correlation between risk-free rates and corporate bond yields, specifically when corporate bonds have callable features. Others such as Longstaff and Schwartz have argued that when the risk-free rate moves higher, the risk-neutral level for the firm's asset value should also be higher. With an exogenously specified default trigger, this implies that the risk-neutral probability of default is lower (i.e., the default risk could be lower). Therefore, the default spread is lower when the risk-free interest rate is higher. It is an academic debate how much the change in the risk-free rate triggers default. What Figure 5.6 does broadly speak to is that when Treasury yields go up, so do corporate and high-yield bond yields. That conclusion emphasizes that a changed, riskier risk-free rate may suggest that when corporate bond spreads are narrow, the compensation for the risk taken may be too low. Figure 5.6 also demonstrates that when that is the case, such as during 1995 to 1997 and 2004 to 2006, the subsequent periods may see much wider corporate bond risk premiums, driven by higher corporate bond yields. Investing in corporate bonds is about credit analysis and understanding of default risk. The corporate bond CDS market is well developed, which allows investors to better gauge expectations of default. Those expectations compared to risk premiums, relative to the overall health of the company and the economy, provides a framework to judge corporate bond investments.

What to Invest In: Non-agency Residential Mortgage-Backed Securities

Residential mortgage-backed securities were the fastest-growing asset class by 2007, but the 2008 crisis shed a negative light on the sector. There are agency and non-agency, known as "private label," securities markets. Non-agency MBS are not guaranteed against defaults of principal or interest. For subprime mortgages, the lifetime default rate on mortgages is estimated to be as high as 80 to 95 percent. For prime mortgages, the estimate is "only" 10 to 25 percent, according to Moody's research. As a result of the default risk, non-agency MBS typically trade at a substantial discount to the remaining principal. Non-agency MBS are issued by private institutions, not by governmental or quasi-governmental agencies.

The underlying collateral generally consists of mortgages that do not conform to the requirements (size, documentation, or loan-to-value ratios) for inclusion in MBS issued by agencies such as Ginnie Mae, Fannie Mae, or Freddie Mac. Prime mortgages are high-quality mortgages that meet stringent underwriting guidelines, similar to those set for agency mortgages by Fannie Mae and Freddie Mac. Subprime mortgages tend to fall into the non-agency market segment because loan balances are greater than those allowed by Fannie and Freddie for conforming loans. Prime mortgage loans have historically carried low default risk and are made to borrowers with good credit records. Alternative-A (Alt-A) mortgages fall between prime and subprime mortgages. The credit scores of these borrowers are typically average or above average, but looser loan documentation requirements or larger loan size disqualify these loans from conforming to Fannie Mae or Freddie Mac underwriting guidelines. Option ARMs are a type of Alt-A loan that is unique because of their flexible repayment.terms. Option ARM mortgages allow for several payment options, including making interest only or less than interest due payments. As a result, the outstanding loan balance can increase over time (negative amortization). These loans were designed to start with an attractively low rate of interest (the "teaser rate") to attract borrowers. Subprime is a class of mortgage extended to borrowers with low credit ratings. In general, these borrowers have damaged credit or limited credit history and provide minimal income and asset verification. Because of the default risk associated with these borrowers, lenders tend to charge a higher interest rate on subprime loans.

Real estate mortgage investment conduits (REMICs) are bonds created from pools of mortgages. Re-REMICs are securities structured from the underlying cash flows of existing REMIC bonds. Dealers create re-REMICs by taking an existing security and placing it in a trust. The trust then issues two new bonds backed by the cash flows of the original security, one bond being senior to the other. The senior bond in the re-REMIC structure receives the credit support that is left on the original bond plus additional credit support in the form of the new subordinate bond issued by the re-REMIC trust to mitigate losses on the collateral.

There are two specific types of securities issued, collateralized mortgage obligations (CMOs) and sequential. A CMO is a security that takes the principal and interest from a pool of assets—mortgage loans, mortgage pass-through securities, or even other CMOs—and allocates those cash flows to different classes or tranches. This is the "waterfall" structure. Planned amortization classes (PAC) are securities where principal is repaid according to a schedule within a specified range of prepayment assumptions called PAC bands or collars. The principal schedule mitigates the risks from average life volatility and reinvestment risk associated with prepayments. Principal schedules are maintained by redirecting unscheduled cash flow to support bonds. The average life is less volatile with prepayment speeds outside the bands because the supports continue to provide stability. The "supports" provide extension or call protection to other scheduled classes in the deal (PACs, PAC IIs, and targeted amortization classes, or "TACs"). If the underlying loan collateral prepays faster than the upper PAC bands, the supports receive all excess principal cash flow. If the collateral prepays more slowly than the lower PAC bands, the supports receive no principal cash flow at all until the PAC schedule is met. When cash flows are called "sequential," the collateral principal payments are reallocated sequentially into a series of short-, intermediate-, and long-maturity bonds. The shorter average life sequential bonds (that pay before the longer sequential bonds within the structure) provide prepayment protection for the longer average life sequential bonds. They also have a shorter principal window than the underlying collateral. There is also the "last cash flow," otherwise known as the "Z tranche." These securities pay no interest until the principal payment window starts, and interest due is added to the outstanding principal of the bond. This is called Z accretion. This means that coupon payments are automatically reinvested at the bond's coupon, and they receive principal payments and interest when other bonds are retired. An addition of the Z bond to a structure can improve the convexity that measures the change in duration (interest rate sensitivity) of the other bonds by reducing extension risk.

In both the agency and the non-agency MBS market, CMOs and sequential paying cash flows are widely traded. In the capital structure—the waterfall—there is a wide variety of bonds to choose from. For a more conservative investor, one would seek the senior cash flow that has sufficient credit support and is backed by additional overcollateralization. A more risk-taking investor would look at the lower part of the waterfall, where subordinated cash flows provide higher returns. What should be realized is that the stated yield on a CMO or MBS security is not a fixed return. Rather, due to prepayment risk and cumulative loss projections, the yield as well as the maturity of the MBS can greatly vary. The underlying collateral is very important too. Fortunately, due to regulatory requirements, information about the underlying collateral has significantly improved. What to look for when analyzing the underlying collateral is the types of borrowers, their delinquency and payment history, the loan-to-value and debt-to-income ratios, and credit scores (FICO). In the United States, there is still a decent amount of issuance in agency MBS markets, as Freddie Mac and Fannie Mae have a very large market share in mortgage origination. The non-agency MBS market, however, has seen its volumes in securitization drastically decline since 2008. Specifically, the non-agency MBS market is likely to remain muted in securitization volumes for the next few years. From the peak in 2007, when the market stood at $2.2 trillion, the universe of non-agency MBS bonds has shrunk to less than $1 trillion. This is shown in Figure 5.7.

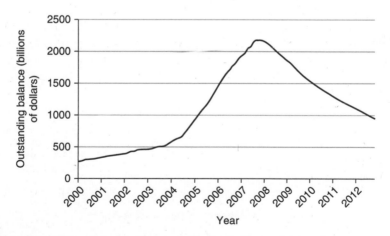

Figure 5.7 The non-agency mortgage-backed securities universe.
(*Source:* Standard & Poor's and Bloomberg.)

Investing in non-agency MBS is tricky. The models used to estimate prepayment speeds and loss projections are complex and showed
serious flaws during 2007 and 2008. It requires a significant amount
of resources to properly analyze the securities. In addition, non-
agency MBS are "unique" securities. They have been issued off specific
"shelves" by banks and by hedge fund and private equity managers.
It requires sifting through the massive amount of securities inventory
to find opportunities. It is important to understand how non-agency
MBS behave in different housing price scenarios. Figure 5.8 shows the
model loss-adjusted spread profile of a non-agency MBS bond at two
different prices. If the bond price appreciates from $42 to $47 and there
is no change in the housing price appreciation scenario, the model loss-
adjusted spread will decline by approximately 250 basis points. On the
other hand, an improvement in the base case housing price appreciation scenario from −6 to 0 percent over the next 2 years may result in
an increase in 175 basis points in loss-adjusted spread. This example
shows that non-agency MBS are highly negatively convex to prepayment speeds when house prices change.

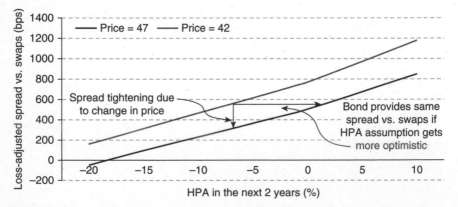

Figure 5.8 Home price appreciation (HPA) and non-agency mortgage-
backed securities performance. bps, basis points.

(*Source:* Bloomberg, Pacific Investment Management Company, PIMCO.)

What to Invest In: New Frontier Markets

Emerging market (EM) corporate, quasi-sovereign, and government debt has been favored by investors over the past few years. The higher real returns, the relative stability of financial systems, solid growth prospects with lower inflation, credible central banks, and the upgrade of credit ratings are among the reasons for favorable demand for the asset class. Evolution of new benchmark indices that use gross domestic product (GDP) weights rather than market weights has typically let EM countries play a greater role in the index universe. EM local currency government yields have behaved more like safe haven yields since 2008. Instead of rising, they have at times fallen in response to worsening global risk sentiment. However, EM local currency government bond yields could be susceptible to adverse external shocks. Moreover, the international role of EM local currency bonds depends crucially on the behavior of exchange rates. In this respect, local emerging sovereign bonds have a multitude of more visible risks, including exchange rate, political, default, and liquidity, to name a few. In Figure 5.9 on page 158, it's shown how local, emerging bond returns compare to other returns.

Research has shown that in general, shocks to the global economy tend to have large effects on the returns of EM bonds. For instance, focusing on the period after the Russian default in 1998, researchers Gonzalez-Rozada and Yeyati (2008) show that about 50 percent of the long-run variability of EM foreign currency sovereign spreads was explained by two main factors: (1) international risk appetite measured by U.S. corporate bond spreads and (2) bond market liquidity measured by the change in U.S. Treasury yields. Domestic factors are also at work. Based on a quantity of flows, the IMF estimates that foreign inflows to EM bonds can be significant at times. Local emerging currency bonds, unlike foreign currency bonds such as U.S. Treasuries, are exposed to cross-border investors that are very sensitive to the risk of unexpected exchange rate changes. Exchange rate fluctuations can drive a large wedge between the hedged and unhedged returns of local emerging

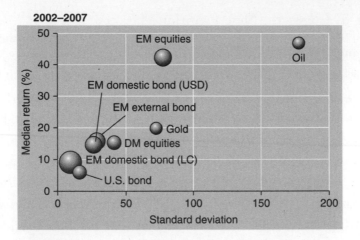

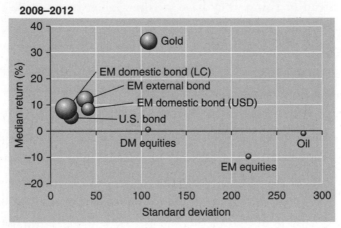

Figure 5.9 Emerging market (EM) local sovereign bond returns versus U.S. Treasuries. DM, developed markets; LC, local markets.

(*Source:* Bank of International Settlements.)

bonds. In a BIS study (2012), the currency effect was simulated in a portfolio context, which includes U.S. Treasuries, equities in advanced markets, oil, and gold. The portfolio weights were determined by the annualized volatility of returns of the individual assets. When EM local currency government bonds were added to the portfolio, the Sharpe ratio, the ratio of excess return over the risk-free rate divided by return volatility (standard deviation of returns), has changed. Table 5.1 displays the portfolio results. From 2003 to 2007 under the assumption that exchange rate risk was fully hedged, the Sharpe ratio of the portfolio did improve by reducing return volatility; however, the diversification gain was marginal. When looking at the period of 2008 to 2012, the addition of local EM bonds to the portfolio nearly doubled the Sharpe ratio. By contrast, the case for diversification appears to be rather weak for the currency unhedged portfolio. From 2003 to 2007, the unhedged portfolio gained very little from diversifying into EM local currency bonds. Between 2008 and 2012, a period of a large depreciation of EM currencies occurred. The portfolio performance was poor (column 5 in Table 5.1), and the Sharpe ratio fell from 3.19 to 1.21. This example shows that high volatility of EM currencies can erode diversification benefits from EM local currency bonds.

Because of their generally strong performance, market participants and commentators have argued that local EM bonds may have become a new source of perceived "safety." This safe haven status remains debatable. The evidence from the BIS shows that EM local government yields have tended to fall in reaction to global risk aversion over the past few years. This contrasts with a situation in which deteriorating risk appetite saw poor performance and a surge in domestic EM government bond yields. The EM local currency bond market is getting "internationalized" as a result of large foreign inflows into EM local currency bonds funds driven by a search for yield. The BIS empirical research results showed that during the global monetary easing cycle between 2009 and 2012, at least a quarter of the decline in domestic EM government bond yields was attributed to lower U.S. Treasury yields. An important implication is that any sign of reversal in super easy global monetary policies could adversely affect EM local currency bonds, as well as capital flows to EMs. The behavior of exchange rates is crucial, especially with regard to unanticipated exchange rate changes. Abrupt and excessive exchange rate changes in EMs can adversely affect their newly found international

Table 5.1 Portfolio Simulation with Emerging Market Local Currency Bonds

	2003–2007			2008–2012		
	Benchmark	Add EM Local Currency Government Bonds . . .		Benchmark	Add EM Local Currency Government Bonds . . .	
		. . . with Currency Risk	. . . without Currency Risk		. . . with Currency Risk	. . . without Currency Risk
Average (= a)	8.9	10.2	8.9	8.3	8.3	7.9
Standard dev. (= b)	2.8	3.2	2.6	6.7	6.8	3.6
Sharpe ratio (= a/b)	3.14	3.19	3.35	1.23	1.21	2.23

a, annual return of the portfolio; b, portfolio annual volatility; EM, emerging market.
(*Source:* Bank for International Settlements.)

role. Typically in response, EM central banks often fall back on official currency market intervention. This can create the perceptions of exchange rate misalignment; as a result, EM currencies may become more volatile in response to new global economic shocks in the future. It is a still a long way to the development of deep and liquid local currency bond markets like the U.S. Treasury market. Even though local EM bonds are viewed as the "new risk-free rates," given the risks outlined, it would be naïve to assume that they provide superior diversification benefits. That said, local EM bonds are perhaps the new frontier bond markets where investors may continue to seek higher returns.

What to Invest In: Treasury Inflation-Protected Securities

The Treasury Inflation-Protected Securities (TIPS) market has grown rapidly over the past few years. Instruments such as TIPS are designed to protect against the negative effects of higher inflation. The coupon interest received is fixed, but the notional principal of the bond is linked to inflation, as measured by the consumer price index (CPI). Thus, when the CPI rises on the month by one tenth of a percent, the notional value of the TIPS goes up by that amount, with a 3-month accretion lag. In the process, the investor accrues interest based on an increased inflation-adjusted principal. In the case of deflation, the principal adjusts for deflation and pays interest on the below-par inflation-adjusted principal. This is also known as the deflation floor. The floor "guarantees" the holder of TIPS the greater of the inflation-adjusted principal or par value at maturity, whichever is higher. The volatility of TIPS has been known to be lower than that of nominal Treasury bonds because of the risk-premium component difference. The nominal bond yield could be viewed as the sum of the real yield (yield adjusted for inflation), an inflation expectation, and the uncertainty of inflation expectations. The yield on TIPS is called real yield, the yield based on the present value that is adjusted for inflation. For nominal Treasury

Table 5.2   Index Returns Compared

Year	Nominal Treasury Index (%)	TIPS Index (%)
1997	9.60	2.40
1998	11.20	3.90
1999	−6.20	2.70
2000	14.30	13.40
2001	6.00	7.10
2002	12.30	17.10
2003	3.30	9.40
2004	2.70	9.00
2005	1.60	2.90
2006	3.10	0.30
2007	9.90	11.00
2008	21.20	−3.00
2009	−9.60	12.10
2010	7.20	6.40
2011	15.80	13.70
2012	2.60	7.70

(*Sources:* Barclays and Bloomberg. Index returns by Barclays.)

bonds the change in the risk-free rate could have a measurable effect on the break-even inflation and the expectation of future inflation implied by TIPS. If one were to look at the U.S. TIPS historical performance in Table 5.2, the first conclusion is that TIPS tend to perform similar to nominal Treasury bonds. There are exceptions, such as in 1999 and 2009, when Treasury bonds sold off because of interest rate hikes and a growing economy, TIPS performed better as realized CPI inflation rose by 1.5 percent. In 2008, it was the opposite because after Lehman's failure, deflation expectations rose sharply and TIPS underperformed nominal Treasuries.

The reasons listed (growth, inflation, and deflation) are part of a natural relationship between TIPS and Treasuries. What has yet to be seen is when Treasury rates go higher because of the risk factors outlined in Chapter 4, specifically when risk perceptions of debt dynamics change. In that case, TIPS are not necessarily a better alternative risk-free rate because uncontrollable government debt would weigh heavily on the economy and is likely to cause deflation rather than inflation.

What to Invest In: Municipal Bonds

By 2010, an intense debate ignited as to whether the U.S. municipal bond market would be the next domino to fall in the financial crisis. Meredith Whitney said in December 2010 that about "fifty to a hundred counties, cities, and towns in the United States" would have "significant" municipal bond defaults, totaling "hundreds of billions" of dollars in losses and that this would be "something to worry about within the next 12 months." The defaults did not materialize, and by late 2012, the $3.7 trillion municipal bond market had enjoyed a significant rally. In terms of defaults, there were five recorded in 2012 (1.8 percent of rated issues), and historically only 71 Moody's-rated bonds and 47 Standard & Poor's (S&P)-rated bonds have defaulted since 1970. The defaults thus far have been centered on smaller areas where the real estate bust had a big impact on local communities.

The financial health of municipalities also seems to have improved since the crisis. According to the Bureau of Economic Analysis and the Census Bureau, state and local government spending, adjusted for inflation, fell 2.7 percent in 2012. Against this, tax receipts and revenues were up by roughly 8 percent versus the prior year. State and local governments, required by law to balance their budgets, always make bond payments a priority. They can do so by cutting spending, raising taxes, reaching agreements on pension entitlements, or refinancing. Default risk seems low for municipal bonds, but that is not to say that they are a substitute for government bonds. As is well known, municipal bonds provide tax exemption from federal taxes and may provide tax exemption from state and local taxes. The latter depends on the investors' residency and the laws in each state. Municipal bonds may also be subject to the alternative minimum tax (AMT).

There are two basic types of municipal bonds. There is a "general obligation bond," whereby principal and interest are secured by the full faith and credit of the issuer and are typically approved by voters as a bond measure. There are also "revenue bonds" that have principal and interest secured by revenues derived from tolls, charges, or rents from the facility built with the proceeds of the bond issue. Public projects financed by revenue bonds include toll roads, bridges, airports, water and sewage treatment facilities, hospitals, and subsidized housing. Many of these bonds are issued by special authorities created for that particular purpose. There are also taxable municipal bonds called Build America Bonds (BABs) that carry special tax credits and federal subsidies for either the bond issuer or the bondholder. BABs are no longer being issued but are available in the secondary market. Other kinds of taxable municipal bonds are those used to fund private projects. They are most often used to fund projects that are not public but private and are sometimes called "private activity bonds." These bonds are subject to federal income tax unless they fall into specific defined categories. Most private activity bonds are subject to the AMT.

There are differences, however, and qualified private activity bonds issued by a governmental unit could be exempt from federal taxes. The reason is that these bonds are financing services or facilities that may be defined as "private" but would be needed by a local or state government. Taxes can impact the opportunity cost of money such as inflation. When interest is tax deductible, there is an incentive for borrowing because it reduces future tax bills. The after-tax cost of borrowing can decline when tax rates increase, and a borrower would be willing to pay a higher interest rate because the after-tax interest rate would stay the same. A simple example is, say a borrower is in the 20 percent tax bracket. A 10 percent loan would have an after-tax interest cost of 8 percent. If the tax rate rises to, for example, 50 percent, the borrower could afford to pay up to 16 percent to have the same after-tax interest cost of 8 percent. When reasoned from a lender's point of view, if tax rates go up, the lender would require a higher pretax coupon interest to keep the same after-tax interest income. Thus, both the borrower and the lender are amenable to interest rate change when taxes rise, and as a result, markets will price this into spreads. The easiest way to look at this is the yield spread between taxable bonds (Treasuries, corporate bonds) and tax-exempt bonds. Whereas a fall in taxes would narrow the spread, a rise in tax rates could widen the spread.

For every investor, an effective comparison would be to look at real after-tax return on a taxable and tax-exempt security. Taxes reduce the net income on taxable bonds, meaning that a tax-exempt municipal bond has a higher after-tax yield than a corporate or Treasury bond that has the same coupon rate. This is a mathematical relationship between the yield of a municipal bond, which equals the yield of the comparable corporate or Treasury bond times 1 minus the marginal tax rate. Thus, for example, when a corporate bond pays 6 percent and the marginal tax rate is 38 percent, the yield on a municipal bond is 3.7 percent (6% * 1 − 38%). This yield generates an equal after-tax interest income stream as a corporate bond earning 6 percent. The tax rate at which an investor would be indifferent between a corporate and municipal bond would be tax rate = 1 − municipal yield/corporate yield. Hence, an investor can make a trade-off between municipal bonds and other bonds by using the marginal tax rate as its equilibrium rate. This way, a taxable equivalent yield of municipal bonds can be calculated by dividing the municipal bond yield by 1 minus the tax rate. There is a municipal bond arbitrage by comparing municipal bonds with corporate bonds with the same maturity, rating, and perhaps even state issued where the corporation is located. There is another comparison when valuing municipal bonds off the risk-free rate. Similar to the federal government, state municipalities have a budget deficit (or surplus), a debt-to-state GDP ratio, and a primary surplus (or deficit).

Table 5.3   U.S. Local States versus the United States

	Average Interest (%)	Equilibrium Interest (%)*	Tax-Equivalent Interest (%)†
Municipal debt	4.9	5.8	8.0
Treasury debt	2.4	−2.7	2.4

*Equilibrium interest = (primary balance/debt-to-GDP ratio) * 100 + real GDP.
†Tax equivalent interest = municipal debt average interest/(1 − marginal tax rate).
(*Sources:* U.S. Census Bureau, Bloomberg, and Standard & Poor's.)

Rating agency Standard & Poor's calculated municipal state bond indices. Table 5.3 shows the weighted average coupon of U.S. states versus the coupon of outstanding U.S. Treasury debt. Municipal debt interest is higher than Treasury debt because not every state and local issue is rated equally.

The municipal equilibrium interest rate is based on the same calculation presented in Chapters 1 and 4. The primary balance is the government's net borrowing or net lending, excluding interest payments on consolidated government liabilities. A federal budget that achieves primary balance has federal revenues equaling spending, but the budget deficit remains as a result of interest payments on past debt. These interest payments can balloon if the average interest cost of the debt rises too quickly or stays consistently above GDP. In the case of municipal state and local debt, even though the interest is higher than that on Treasury debt, the higher equilibrium interest implies that it has better finances, that is, a primary surplus (small) and a low debt-to-GDP ratio. The federal government is the opposite: it has a primary deficit and a rising debt-to-GDP ratio. Negative equilibrium interest suggests that current interest rates are too high and could start adding to the growing debt burden. Municipal bond investors should actively analyze state and local debt finances to determine whether the equilibrium interest rate is below or above the tax-equivalent interest rate. The debate about whether more defaults will occur on a local and state level may not have highlighted enough the fact that interest cost and local and state debt-to-GDP ratios are low. For this reason alone, municipal bonds are credits and cannot be seen as a substitute for Treasury bonds. The tax advantage comparison should be incorporated whether a specific municipality has a higher or lower equilibrium interest than Treasury or corporate bonds.

What to Invest In: Interest Rate Parity and Currencies

One of the other oldest standing ideas in finance and economics is the interest rate parity relationship. The parity is such that there is a no-arbitrage condition that presents on equilibrium at which investors will be indifferent to interest available on bank deposits, bonds, or loans in two countries. In practice, this condition does not always hold. It allows for potential opportunities to earn "riskless" profits from the interest rate parity, known as covered interest arbitrage. Of course, such arbitrage would work only if one can access markets without constraints. Thus, two working assumptions are capital mobility and perfect substitutability of assets in two countries. For currencies, the interest rate parity condition implies that the expected return on domestic assets should equal the expected return on assets in foreign currency, adjusted for transaction costs. If the parity holds, investors cannot automatically pocket a profit by borrowing in a country with a lower interest rate and reinvesting in a foreign country with a higher interest rate.

There is risk involved, such as losses from exchanging domestic currency as well as transaction tax changes and market liquidity. Two forms are generally described. The first is the uncovered interest rate parity, in which exposure to foreign exchange risk can be very high because of unanticipated changes in exchange rates. The covered interest rate parity is the hedged version, in which a forward or futures contract has been used to minimize the exchange rate risk. The empirical evidence has been mixed. Results have been the strongest when uncovered interest rate parity and purchasing power parity hold together. When that is the case, the relationship is about the "real interest rate parity." This suggests that expected real interest rates represent expected adjustments in the real exchange rate. There is proof that this relationship generally holds strongly over longer terms and among EM countries. In principle, many central banks see a weaker currency as a convenient way of achieving objectives, especially when other tools are limited. Exchange rate targeting could be seen as another form of "reflation" when central banks actively pursue a weaker currency. Responding to one another's policy actions with "soft" currency pegging creates, to a degree, a semi-fixed exchange rate mechanism. Within such a system, central banks that strive to achieve stable inflation via "reflation" led by a weaker currency may experience real effective exchange variability. Hence, the real interest rate parity relationship is important for investors to watch. Specifically, when investing in currencies, the "carry" component is what the interest rate parity addresses. The interest rate differential between countries can drive capital flows and thereby the value of the exchange rate. What is often applied in global portfolio management is a currency overlay or currency basket strategy. This is an enhanced return strategy whereby a group of currencies is chosen based on valuation, fundamentals, risks, and interest rate differentials. Such a strategy involves going "long" higher-yielding currencies and "short" lower-yielding currencies. By deploying the strategy, a total return index can be calculated. Figure 5.10 on page 169 displays the strategy for emerging and developed (G10) markets.

With interest rate differentials narrowed to close to zero for the developed world, currency returns in G10 may become more difficult. The total return index for G10 shows a 5.6 percent return for the period of 2000 to 2012 with a standard deviation of above 10 percent and a Sharpe ratio of 0.5, according to Bloomberg data. For EM, the return was not too different at 6.5 percent with a standard deviation over 12 percent. Both demonstrate how currency returns have narrowed

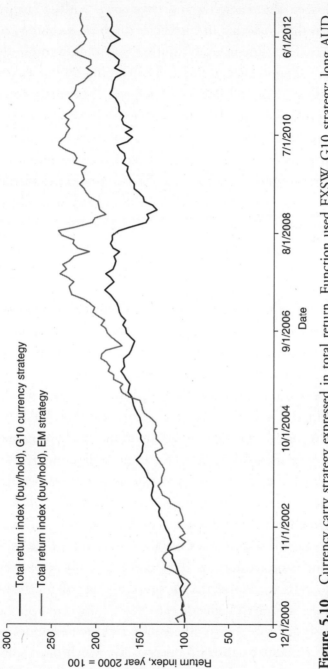

Figure 5.10 Currency carry strategy expressed in total return. Function used FXSW. G10 strategy: long AUD, NZD, NOK/short EUR, JPY, and CHF. Emerging markets strategy: long BRL, TRY, INR/short EUR, JPY, and CHF. Total return index = interest rate return + spot return. EM, emerging market.

(Source: Bloomberg.)

169

over time between the emerging and developed worlds. For investors, this means that investing in currencies can be less counted on to earn the interest rate difference, but rather may require more directional bets on the spot exchange rate. That means having a far better understanding of capital flows in foreign exchange markets and understanding of economic and political factors. In addition, one has to be willing to accept more volatility to achieve returns in foreign exchange. For a currency basket of high- and low- to zero-yielding currencies to be profitable investors may be forced to select currencies with higher interest rates that are less liquid and perhaps subject to greater domestic capital controls.

What to Invest In: How About Equities?

Numerous studies have compared long-term returns between stocks and bonds. Noted academics such as Robert Shiller and Roger Ibbotson have researched extensively associated equity and market risk premiums. A basic conclusion from this research can be drawn: equities always outperform bonds over the long run, albeit with periods of extreme volatility. To visualize, one way to show that this holds true is to look at the historical equity risk premium of the S&P 500 index and the long-term Treasury yield, adjusted for annual inflation. Figure 5.11 on page 171 shows that with long bond real yields near zero and their average around 4.5 percent, the equity real earnings yield is around 5 percent (below the historical average of 6.9 percent). It is a striking aspect of today's investment universe, the wide difference between equity and bond expected returns. The return gap, also known as the "equity risk premium," is near the historical average of 5 percent for the United States as seen in Figure 5.11.

There are several reasons why the equity risk premium is so high. For one, there remains heightened uncertainty, which has made risk aversion almost a permanent state of mind. As previously mentioned,

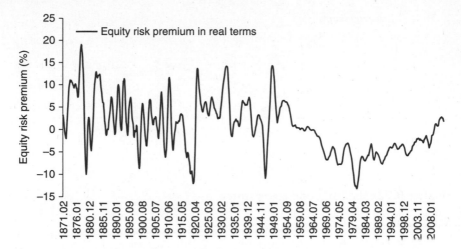

Figure 5.11 Equity risk premium, long bond real yield, and equity real earnings yield. Inflation is measured by year over year % change of the consumer price index (CPI). Equity real earnings yield = 1/price-earnings (PE) ratio adjusted for CPI y/y%, long bond real yield = 30-year Treasury bond yield adjusted for CPI y/y%. Equity risk premium = earnings yield − bond yield. Monthly data for 1871 to 2012.

(*Source:* Robert Shiller, *Irrational Exuberance*, 2nd ed. [Princeton, NJ: Princeton University Press, 2005].)

there are central bank activism, subtle forms of financial repression, and scarcity of AAA government bonds. All of these factors have made bond yields excessively low. On the other hand, equity returns are high, stimulated by quantitative easing, as well as significantly improved margins because of effective corporate cost control. This situation has created a new kind of "teeter totter" between bond and stock expected returns relative to market beta, displayed in Figure 5.12 on page 172. Based on the comparisons in Figures 5.11 and 5.12, one may draw the conclusion that bonds are "overvalued" and stocks are "undervalued." That is not necessarily true. For one thing, the demand for bonds may have a structural nature. Since 2009, the divergence between stock indices and bond yields has been extraordinary. The stock market's performance implies what is known as a "V-shape" economic recovery;

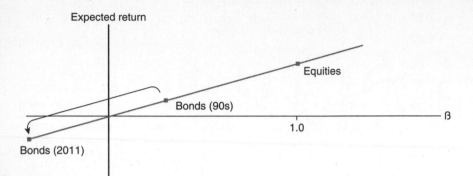

Figure 5.12   Equity-bond teeter totter.
(*Source:* Barclays Equity Gilt Study 2011.)

low bond yields imply a U-shape or worse L-shape recovery. As
Figure 5.12 shows, the expected returns of bonds have shifted down
versus their market beta; it is the opposite for equities. An explanation
is that although equity prices reflect a stronger recovery sometime in
the future, ultra-low bond yields are a product of a consensus view that
the output and unemployment gap remains so large that it continues
to create disinflationary forces in goods, services, prices, and wages.
This may keep Federal Reserve policy on hold for a long time. As a
result, a more consistent equity risk premium near 5 percent may not
be entirely unrealistic.

An important question is when the teeter totter in Figure 5.12
shifts and bond expected returns rise relative to those of equities.
This depends on a few factors. Historically, the correlation between
stocks and bonds from 1930s to 2008 has been moderately negative
to zero, according to Bloomberg data. Since 2009, that correlation
has decisively turned positive to about 0.6, in part because of significant influence by central banks on government bond yields. Thus, the
correlation's falling back to zero would be a signal of renormalization
between equity and bond expected returns that could result into a
lower equity risk premium. Another factor to consider is the cost of

equity and the cost of debt. Both determine the weighted average cost of capital (WACC). New York University estimated that the WACC for the different sectors in the S&P 500 is around 7 percent, and the average return on equity (ROE) is around 15 percent, according to Bloomberg data. If the WACC were to rise above ROE, expected returns on equities may have significant downside. To be sure, one has to look at the dynamics of the change in WACC. The debt component of the WACC is partly determined by the level of the risk-free rate, with a risk premium added that is typically taken from corporate bond spreads or CDS. If the risk-free rate were to rise materially while corporate bonds stay in demand, the narrowing of corporate bond spreads in that case could lower the WACC. Here, too, the spread between ROE and WACC may remain wider, an indication that expected returns for equities stay under the influence of a distorted risk-free rate.

There are many forecasts and estimates of what the future holds for stock returns. The sharp fall in yields of safe haven assets has raised a few questions among many in the financial industry. Negative real yields on government bonds and now, in some cases, on high-quality corporate credit as well as investors with a broad investment mandate wondering why one would still own such securities because they have, after tax and adjusted for inflation, a negative return. The question is an interesting one because while these securities have become more expensive, safe haven assets have also become more effective in mitigating portfolio risk. Safe havens look more like a mark-to-market insurance contract than a traditional store of value. To compare expected returns between safe haven bonds such as Treasuries and stock returns, the "cyclically adjusted PE ratio" by Shiller may provide insight. This price-to-earnings (P/E) ratio uses a trailing 10-year average of reported earnings to smooth out their cyclical volatility (earnings can be twice as volatile as the equity prices). Figure 5.13 on page 174 shows that based on Shiller's estimate, the cyclically adjusted P/E ratio is at 21 versus 14 for the actual ratio of the S&P 500 index at the end of 2012.

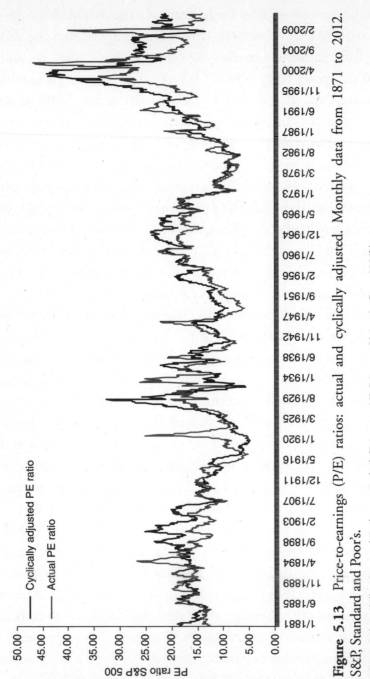

Figure 5.13 Price-to-earnings (P/E) ratios: actual and cyclically adjusted. Monthly data from 1871 to 2012. S&P, Standard and Poor's.

(*Source:* Robert Shiller, *Irrational Exuberance*, 2nd ed. [Princeton, NJ: Princeton University Press, 2005].)

Projected 5 years forward, the compounded annual growth rate of the cyclically adjusted P/E ratio is 7.5 percent, adjusted for annual 2012 inflation. This number presents a forward return on the broader stock index that may not necessarily materialize. But it does say that, based on low interest rates, the excess return premium demanded on stocks is higher than that on bonds. For example, from 1945 to 1970, when real interest rates were on average −2 percent, the average historical CAGR 5 years and 10 years projected forward was around 3 to 4 percent adjusted for inflation. That excess premium of 6 percent is similar to that during the recent period of 2008 to 2012, when real interest rates were also −2 percent. The historical comparison suggests two things. Negative real interest rates generate higher P/E multiples as the free cash flow improves because of a lower discount rate. P/E multiple expansions are also caused by uncertainty that expresses itself in lower interest rates. This is a result of an unusual time when individual investors remain sidelined. Assets in equity mutual, exchange-traded, and closed-end funds have increased in market value by about 85 percent to $5.6 trillion since the recovery in stocks began in March 2009, trailing the S&P 500 Index's 94 percent advance, according to data compiled by Bloomberg and Morningstar, Inc. From a variety of surveys by Morningstar and other mutual fund providers, it appears that individuals are cutting the proportion of their assets in stocks. The percentage of households owning stock mutual funds has also fallen, dropping every year since 2008 to 46.4 percent in 2011, the second lowest since 1997, according to the 2012 Investment Company Institute's (ICI) annual mutual fund survey. The technology bubble in the 1990s saw equity mutual funds expand twice as much as the S&P 500. Stocks' representation in 401(k) and individual retirement account funds rose to about 90 percent in 2000 from 77 percent in 1992. That money has since gone to the relative safety of fixed income investments, with nearly $1 trillion having gone into bond funds since March 2009, according to ICI data.

Implied Returns from Cash Flow Multiples

In Finance 101, free cash flow is assumed to grow at a constant rate in perpetuity beyond the explicit forecast period. Its continuing value is the value of a growing perpetuity. This can be expressed by using a multiple of free cash flow that is as follows:

$$\text{Free cash flow multiple} = \frac{(1 + \text{growth})}{(\text{Weighted average cost of capital} - \text{growth})}$$

This multiple is entirely determined by the growth rate and the cost of capital. There is no forecast period assumed, but the exercise demonstrates how a change in the risk-free rate influences the multiple. Assuming for a moment that the broader stock index represents the entire free cash flow generated in the economy, the multiple can be approximated by the index P/E ratio. Estimating the WACC is a rudimentary experiment. For the cost of equity following the capital asset pricing model (CAPM) approach, the equity risk premium is around 4.8 percent using Shiller's historical data. The cost of debt is assumed to be the risk-free rate—in this case, the 10-year U.S. Treasury yield. Under different growth assumptions, the cash flow multiple can be calculated using the simplified WACC. By using the formula presented in Chapters 1 and 4, a "new" risk-free rate can be calculated that would adjust the WACC. Table 5.4 shows that the WACC with the adjusted risk-free rate rises well above the WACC with the old risk-free rate, and, not surprisingly, the free cash flow multiple falls. This is no doubt a theoretical example. The idea, however, is to show that the embedded risk premium in the risk-free rate increases implied returns demanded, measured by 1/free cash flow multiple.

Does this mean that stock investing is not attractive? No. A "new" risk-free rate implying higher than present rates means that stock valuation and selection should include a few requirements. An investor should look at companies that have high free cash flow, a stable

**Table 5.4   Free Cash Flow Multiples Under the Old
and New Risk-Free Rates***

GDP Growth				
	1%	2%	3%	4%
WACC with old risk-free rate (%)	Cash Flow Multiples			
8.70	13	15	18	22
9.50	12	14	16	19
10.70	10	12	13	16
11.10	10	11	13	15
GDP Growth				
	1%	2%	3%	4%
WACC with adjusted risk-free rate (%)	Cash Flow Multiples			
13.0	8	9	10	12
13.8	8	9	10	11
14.5	7	8	9	10
15.7	7	7	8	9

GDP, gross domestic product.
*The new risk-free rate formula is R(f) = primary balance (t)/debt-to-GDP ratio * 100 + growth rate.
The weighted average cost of capital (WACC) assumes a 50/50 weight between debt and equity, equity
risk premium of 4.8 percent based on Shiller history, and risk-free rate of 10-year Treasury yield.
(*Sources:* Robert Shiller, *Irrational Exuberance*, 2nd ed. [Princeton, NJ: Princeton University Press, 2005];
Bloomberg; Organisation for Economic Co-operation and Development; and International Monetary
Fund.)

dividend payout ratio, and cash flow multiples that stay in a range
under different WACC and growth scenarios. To find these companies, an investor has to become a stock picker through a thorough
method of bottom-up analysis. To start with, one should make an
inventory of a company's income statement, balance sheet, and "return
on invested capital" (ROIC), the ratio of net operating profits after
taxes (NOPAT) divided by invested capital. NOPAT is calculated as
reported net income plus the sum of goodwill, interest expense, and
tax paid minus the sum of investment and interest income and the
tax shield from interest expense. Invested capital represents all of the
cash that debt holders and shareholders have invested in the company.

Invested capital can be calculated by subtracting cash and equivalents and non-interest-bearing current liabilities from total assets. When calculating the ROIC and subtracting the WACC, the difference indicates how much an investor would incrementally earn as the company is creating value. The assumption of the risk-free rate plays a key role. Studies (e.g., Ibbotson, 2000) have shown that stock prices are highly correlated with the difference between ROIC and WACC. Value creation is the key, and simply looking at earnings per share or net income does not indicate whether a company creates value. Furthermore, high sales growth can be harmful when new capital is being invested in value-destroying projects. An advantage of using ROIC is that measures such as earnings per share (EPS), net income, and growth do not tell how much capital is required to generate those numbers. ROIC can also be used to understand why stocks trade at different multiples such as P/E, enterprise value/invested capital (EV/IC), or price-to-book value (P/B). The P/E ratio is a function of not only growth but also ROIC. Generally speaking, companies with higher ROICs seem to have more value. The trend of ROIC may be an advanced indicator signaling that a company is having an easy or hard time dealing with competition.

How to Invest: Exchange-Traded Funds

Building a portfolio of individual covered, corporate, mortgage, and TIPS bonds and stocks takes time and resources. For an individual investor, this is not impossible, but the transaction costs and fees can sometimes be high. Fortunately, the evolution of financial markets has created exchange-traded funds (ETFs). These are investment vehicles that have many attributes of mutual funds but trade throughout the day on an exchange like a stock. ETFs come in a variety of styles, including passive or index ETFs, which typically aim to closely track their underlying index. There are actively managed ETFs, which are managed with the objective of providing above-benchmark returns or objectives such as income or total return. ETFs offer investors many benefits, such as intraday liquidity and pricing, trading flexibility, transparency of holdings, and potential tax advantages. Because ETFs trade like stocks, investors may be able to buy them on margin or sell them short, and have the added flexibility to use limit or stop-loss orders and, in many cases, use options strategies. Most ETFs are open-end investment companies that are registered under the Investment Company Act of 1940 and are subject to essentially the same rules and regulations as traditional mutual funds. They are investment vehicles in which investors own a proportional share of the pooled underlying securities.

Unlike mutual funds, which issue shares in the fund directly to investors and redeem them at the net asset value (NAV) determined at the end of each trading day, ETFs trade throughout the day on exchanges at current market prices. ETF shares are issued or redeemed through an authorized participant (AP) in what is called a "creation or redemption." An ETF creation is the process by which APs—self-clearing broker–dealers who have signed an agreement with the ETF manager—deliver the securities or cash that constitute the creation basket of the ETF to the fund manager in exchange for units of the ETF. Conversely, ETF redemption occurs when an AP delivers shares of the ETF to the fund manager in exchange for the individual securities or cash constituting the fund redemption basket. A creation or redemption basket contains the securities the ETF manager accepts or delivers in exchange for shares of the ETFs. Through creations, the net assets under management (AUM) of the ETF increase in response to demand for the shares, and through redemptions, AUM decline as supply outstrips demand. Creation and redemption transactions occur only at the NAV of the fund and can be implemented only in block unit sizes, which typically range from 50,000 to 100,000 ETF shares. Typically, an ETF manager has several APs who can create or redeem ETFs.

As of the end of 2012, there was \$1.45 trillion invested in ETFs, with 1,276 funds trading. Morningstar is an all-around provider of ETF analysis, including extensive research on the performance of ETFs. On its website under the ETF section, the entire universe is listed in terms of year-to-date and historical performance. Each of the asset classes discussed has specific ETFs traded in the marketplace. For example, for covered bonds, non-agency MBSs, corporate bonds, foreign exchange, TIPS, and EM, each has its own ETFs. Bundling them in one portfolio could be easier and faster for the typical investor than building a portfolio with actual bonds. It would be wise, however, to diversify among ETFs, mutual funds, and individual stocks and bonds. One must realize that assembling different ETFs entails exposure to an underlying reference portfolio. The dynamic changes in that portfolio are reflected on an intraday basis in the pricing of the ETF, another key difference from a mutual fund. There should be a natural arbitrage between an ETF, a mutual fund, and an ETF index. Whereas ETF shares are traded intraday with a value below or above NAV, mutual fund shares strike at end of day NAV. An "arbitrage" is to short the ETF or buy a mutual fund of the same entity to lock in a return differential. Relevant is that ETF shares can be borrowed at low cost (e.g., Fed funds flat), and ETF liquidity is sufficient.

There are a variety of other ETF strategies to consider. For one, there is the portfolio satellite idea of a blend of index and active investing. Index investments, such as ETFs, become the foundation of the portfolio's construction, and actively managed investments are added as satellite positions. With this approach, investors index their core holdings to more efficient asset classes and limit their selection to active managers who hopefully deliver consistent alpha or outperformance for other categories. Today, most large pension plans use a core or satellite approach in their investment policy. ETFs can work as effective hedging tools for managing risk. For example, investors can guard against overconcentrated equity positions by using ETFs as single stock substitutes. This hedging technique can be useful to reduce risk and volatility by letting stockholders diversify away from large equity positions in the companies they own or work at. Also, inverse performing or short ETFs allow investors to hedge against a market decline. ETFs can be leveraged with margin. Margin is borrowing money from a broker to buy securities and involves considerable risk. Minimum maintenance requirements are enforced by FINRA (Financial Industry Regulatory Authority), the New York Stock Exchange, and individual brokerage firms. Although margin investing can be profitable for investors who are correct about the direction of their holdings, the interest charges or borrowing costs can adversely affect returns.

ETF investors have a multiplicity of option strategies at their disposal. An options investor can control a large amount of ETF shares by paying a premium. The premium price is a fraction of what it would cost to purchase the shares in the open market. This provides an options investor with a great deal of leverage and a high risk-reward opportunity. A more defensive approach uses put options in conjunction with portfolio holdings. Buying protective puts on ETF positions would help guard a portfolio against declining prices. There are many other tactical possibilities with options. However, there are substantial risks involved with options, including liquidity, interest rate, market, credit, management, and the risk that a position cannot be closed when most advantageous. Investors in derivatives could lose more than the amount invested.

ETFs, like individual stocks, can be shorted. Shorting involves selling borrowed shares that an investor does not own in expectation that the price of an ETF will decline in value. If the ETF does decrease in value, it can be bought by the short seller at a lower price, which results in a profit. Shorting individual stocks on a downtick is prohibited, but ETFs are exempt from this rule. This translates into easier and more fluid short selling with ETFs. Note that shorting is an advanced technique and involves substantial risk. For example, the security in theory could rise infinitely, leaving the investor with short exposure, having to buy back the security at a higher price and thus a loss. Convenient market exposure to various industry sectors is readily obtained with ETFs. By tactically shifting assets, investors can over- and underweight specific sectors according to their financial research, economic outlook, or market objective. Owning or selling concentrated business segments allows ETF investors to capitalize on both positive and negative sector trends. Wash-sale rules do not permit investors to realize a stock loss if they repurchase the same stock within 30 days. This problem can be avoided with smart tax loss planning. By redeploying the loss proceeds into an ETF in the same sector as the stock, for example, the wash-sale rule can be avoided. This allows investors to offset any capital gains with capital losses and still maintain market exposure. So with that in mind and the acceptance of a changed risk-free rate, the alternatives presented in this chapter could be considered in ETF form, bearing in mind liquidity, interest rate, and other risks.

Chapter 6

Bubble Management

In an interview on Bloomberg Television in December 2012, Bloomberg surveillance host Thomas Keene asked me the following: "When you look at central banks, they talk about interest rate management. Now we've got the Evans central bank talking about job management. Is Stephen Roach right—right that we've got to have a credit bubble management or a bond bubble management as well?" It was not only an excellent question, but also one for the books. A central bank managing a bubble is one of the core ideas about the "end of the risk-free rate thesis." A bubble is about expectations and asset prices. A central bank has to carefully convey a message when expectations are heightened through elevated asset prices. If it does not, the central bank may fall victim to its own policy. Holding a large stock of government bonds on its balance sheet may signal that the central bank sees government bond yields as being low for some time. It also creates lower interest rates than what inflation, growth, or riskier assets may suggest. This artificially depresses risk premiums, something that people such as Alan Greenspan have warned of. In his opening remarks at the Jackson Hole Symposium in 2005, he addressed this issue:

> Vast increase in the market value of asset claims is in part the indirect result of investors accepting lower compensation for risk. Any onset of increased investor caution elevates risk premiums and, as a consequence, lowers and promotes liquidations of the debt that supported asset prices. This is the reason why history has not dealt kindly with the aftermath of protracted periods of low-risk premiums.

The essence of low risk premiums is that there are two sides of the equation. There are risky and "risk-free" returns. Over the course of the preceding chapters, this has been demonstrated with examples. Even though some were theoretical, it is evident that ultra-low interest rates and high asset prices such as stocks versus the sluggish performance of the economy present a "wedge." A pressing question is whether this wedge persists or adjusts. This hinges on whether fundamentals catch up to asset prices and central banks.

Since 2009, central bank policy has been characterized as competitive. One central bank started a large buying program, and others reacted either by incentives or by being forced. Despite significantly tighter risk premiums from 2009 to 2012, there remained fragmentation between market-based and survey-based rates. These are the credit aspects of central bank competition. Most major central banks faced a broken credit transmission mechanism after the financial crisis. To address this, they purchased government debt in large quantities. The other "competitive" aspect is deficits and debt. Each central bank has to deal with private and public sector debt deleveraging to support a process that is as orderly as possible. In this respect, the central bank's bond portfolio has an important function. The interest rate difference earned between the rate on money and the yield on a government bond is known as "carry." This income earned was used as a dividend transfer to the Treasury, which in turn can use the windfall to lower the deficit. Over time, the outstanding debt could be addressed that way, too, albeit at a very slow pace.

Tied into central bank competition are symptoms. Central banks accumulating more government debt has driven the real cost of debt negative. This has diluted incentives on the part of the government to take action, and that has led to greater political standoffs and unwillingness to make difficult choices. Traditionally, a central bank is a lender of last resort. With a large market share in government bonds, the central bank was assigned the task of market maker of last resort. A distinction between lender and market maker of last resort is that between a "bank run" and a "market run." A market run is a synergistic contraction of liquidity across borders among a wide range of market participants, in which perceptions of solvency quickly change because of asset price fluctuations. The narrow gap between liquidity and solvency freezing the interbank market leaves the central bank alone in restoring market functioning. Bank for International Settlements economist William White noted that with many central banks active in different markets, prices will be increasingly determined by central banks' actions. A negative is information about price discovery. Corollary to what the central bank tries to achieve, information provided by asset prices is almost the same information the central bank has generated with its purchases. This argument could be taken further when such "asymmetry" in one market is affecting purchase programs in other markets. Perhaps this could become a principal–agent problem among the central banks themselves. One central bank acts as principal while others remain agents. This dynamic complicates central bank bubble management. To better gauge this complexity, the analysis starts with an understanding of the risk of debt. An investor has to identify measures showing how debt risks can suddenly change through perceptions of confidence. Thorough analysis is needed of who holds government debt and what are their common interests. A set of risk metrics has to be established to determine a fundamental and credit view. These issues are addressed in the following sections.

Debt Confidence

Debt has the ability to provide leverage and deliver destruction. Debt is a liability that does not have flexibility and cannot be adjusted without a breach of contract. Debt payments are a measure of the obligations a debtor must meet. Its steady stream of fixed cash flows is what makes debt attractive to investors, savers, and issuers. This is why debt has been defined as "risk free" when there is no doubt that a debtor would not repay. As argued in the preceding chapters, most government-issued debt has gained the perception of a contingent payoff. That has made it a riskier financial asset for those who own it and a riskier liability for those who owe it. Even if interest rates are low, this does not mean that debt is less risky. In fact, investors are now required to closely monitor a government's finances to establish whether a contingency has occurred. It is also necessary to monitor a governmental debtor's behavior because it can increase the likelihood of more contingencies happening. Often associated with this problem is "moral hazard," wherein a debtor gets bailed out but repeats the behavior, creating another contingent liability that becomes uncontrollable over time.

There are the issues of control and property rights. These have led to lengthy litigation in debt restructurings that has created additional uncertainty. Another situation in which debt can be risky is when there is limited liability or no recourse. Limited liability for corporate equity holders means, for example, that the most they stand to lose financially is the value of their equity stakes. Their other personal resources cannot be called upon to meet the debt obligations of the corporation. This is because debt is senior to equity in the capital structure of a company. For a government, however, debt is a liability that has no limit. In this context, the higher the leverage of an entity that has issued more debt, the closer the definition of debt gets to equity. When debt resembles equity, the uncertainty of debt service can increase, and thereby the likelihood of default. Thus the question about whether we live in an age of a "bond bubble" has to address how much confidence in debt remains, knowing that it has increasingly equity-like characteristics. There are a few recent examples of a confidence breakdown in big sovereign debt markets.

Summer of European Sovereign Discontent

By late June 2011, the European government bond market got caught in a "bank–sovereign loop." Banks sold assets to build up their required capital, and they targeted their sovereign bond holdings. And as sovereign spreads widened, bank stocks fell because banks were large holders of government bonds. The liquidity in the bond market deteriorated, which put more pressure on bank stocks, and banks continued to liquidate government bonds. The loop was profound in 2011 and eroded confidence, partly because wider sovereign spreads also led to bank and sovereign downgrades. This was the backdrop of the European sovereign crisis turning into a global sovereign crisis. Between early July and August 2011, a rapid sequence of events presented a "wake-up call" for governments. The European debt crisis intensified as Greece needed a second bailout. Germany demanded that private sector involvement (PSI) be part of the second package. Portugal, subject to numerous downgrades, got cut to junk status, which led to passive index portfolio liquidations of Portuguese bonds. The developments in Italy took a turn for the worse when then finance minister Tremonti was going to resign. This stemmed from a scandal involving allegations of graft and corruption by one of Tremonti's close advisors. Suddenly, investor confidence "flipped." A contagion effect happened as investors sought to sell the most "rich" instrument in their portfolios that presented the most uncertain market. In this case, it was Italian bonds. In the absence of any official intervention, Italian and other sovereign bond spreads widened sharply. The price action pointed to a mini-panic about Tremonti's resignation that would jeopardize the Italian government's approved new austerity package of tax increases and spending cuts. The measures would eliminate Italy's budget deficit by 2014, but because those were now in doubt, this increased tensions within the coalition government, which spilled over negatively into market sentiment because political instability was associated with Italy's debt sustainability being questioned. When more sovereign downgrades followed—Ireland and the United States—and the European Central Bank amid the turmoil hiked interest rates and made no sign of market intervention, market tensions escalated.

Underneath the tension were technical factors. An intense debate centered on how precisely confidence in Italian bonds was suddenly lost in those early days of July 2011. The confidence change can perhaps not entirely be attributed to selling waves by Scandinavian, Benelux, and Asian end investors and by European banks cutting Italian bond risk from their trading books. In fact, the Bank of Italy's stability report of 2011 highlighted it more precisely. Italian banks in particular relied on their domestic government bond funding market ("repo") to procure uncollateralized funds from parties abroad. When the extension of repo transactions' settlement dates was implemented to avoid failures of collateral delivery, the measure created a longer window of time for domestic Italian banks to sell their Italian government bond holdings. When the penalty for failures was changed, the liquidity disappeared from the funding market. Without a properly functioning repo market, a good part of the "demand destruction" in Italian government bonds really happened at local Italian banks. With Italian banks and the nonfinancial sector representing 50 percent of the Italian bond market, settlement and penalty changes in the domestic funding market brought liquidity and insolvency close together. This is precisely what happened in Greece in May 2010 when its government bond market experienced distress. Also in Greece, repo failure extensions were implemented that led to "forced auctions" (automatic securities lending). These auctions facilitated short selling of Greek government bonds right at the moment when the markets lost confidence in Greece's solvency. Through a process of vicious circles, they created the unique combination of credit and scarcity concerns. This is the technical backdrop to why Italian bonds sold off so rapidly in the summer of 2011. The sell-off undermined the confidence of long-term investors, and they proactively liquidated their Italian bond holdings, anticipating further rating downgrades. Those downgrades were a response to higher Italian bond yields, which in turn were caused by selling waves by investors and banks. This was the process of a vicious circle that created a unique combination of credit and scarcity concerns. This circle or loop is demonstrated in Figure 6.1 on page 190. When stress rose to further extremes, official intervention by European officials finally arrived. Unfortunately, the measures proved to fall short of expectations. On July 21, 2011, European Union leaders released a statement that was full of "sweeteners." These included long-term loans at a low interest rate to Greece coupled with flexible credit lines, a commitment to allow for bank recapitalizations across European countries, and a voluntary Greek debt exchange to provide debt relief. The emergency measures cut the tail of near-term serial defaults in several European countries but failed to get a "bail-in effect" by longer-term investors who had lost confidence in European sovereign debt.

What are the lessons for investors from the "summer of sovereign discontent"? Financial repression through the banking system holding large quantities of government debt can perpetuate a sovereign debt crisis. The vulnerability of the financial system can easily translate negatively to the government backing the system with guarantees. Regular and detailed analysis on government debt holdings across sectors and entities is therefore needed. Any crisis has a "noise factor." To separate

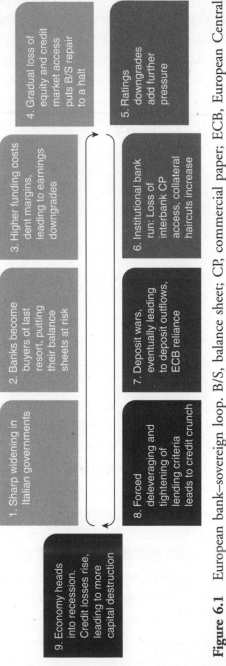

Figure 6.1 European bank–sovereign loop. B/S, balance sheet; CP, commercial paper; ECB, European Central Bank.

(*Source:* Bank Credit Analyst, PIMCO.)

The nine boxes in the loop contain:

1. Sharp widening in Italian governments
2. Banks become buyers of last resort, putting their balance sheets at risk
3. Higher funding costs dent margins, leading to earnings downgrades
4. Gradual loss of equity and credit market access puts B/S repair to a halt
5. Ratings downgrades add further pressure
6. Institutional bank run: Loss of interbank CP access, collateral haircuts increase
7. Deposit wars, eventually leading to deposit outflows, ECB reliance
8. Forced deleveraging and tightening of lending criteria leads to credit crunch
9. Economy heads into recession. Credit losses rise, leading to more capital destruction

the relevant facts from the noise is the hardest thing to do in an investment context. The case of the European debt crisis saw a compounding effect of noise that made the crisis puzzle more complex. Official statements by governments and central banks are places to look for signs of imminent intervention. The technical workings of markets are important, as measures of liquidity and stress have become a much needed tool for portfolio management. Lastly, a crisis is about cause and effect, specifically "unexpected causality." Underlying this concept is the domino theory known as financial domino effects. It is important to recognize the forces that could lead to a sudden chain reaction. These sudden events may lead to a crisis in which the domino effects themselves can accelerate the path of crisis. The three major categories of domino effects are social-political, economic, and financial. The sovereign crisis in Europe had all three categories. To distinguish them allows for a better understanding of the path ahead, the potential range of outcomes, and what policy actions may be expected.

Confidence or Kabuki: Japan

In a 2011 study, the International Monetary Fund (IMF) looked at the risks of the Japanese government bond market, known as Japanese government bonds (JGBs). Japan had been in a secular decline in terms of growth and population after its stock and real estate bubble burst in 1989 to 1991. Since then, yields on JGBs had been falling almost continuously, as shown in Figure 6.2 on page 192. The history shows that the JGB yields were once double digit.

The IMF study emphasized that over the medium term, the domestic Japanese market had less capacity to absorb new JGB debt. The structural factors were that the population was aging and the risk appetite of the younger generation would increase as they had to carry the greater burden of the elderly population. The favorable factors that had supported the JGB market, such as the large pool of domestic

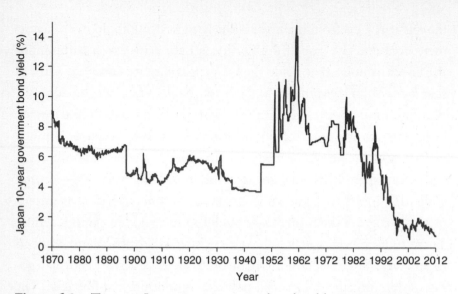

Figure 6.2 Ten-year Japanese government bond yield, 1870 to 2012.
(*Sources:* Merrill Lynch and Bloomberg.)

savings, a captive audience, and a high share of domestic ownership, could diminish. The adverse effect could be that the stock of gross public debt would exceed household financial assets. That presented a potential "tipping point" for Japanese government bonds that could no longer solely rely on domestic financing.

By late 2012, a new Japanese government was elected, and its new leader, Shinzō Abe, pressured the Bank of Japan to take greater easing action by adopting an inflation target of 2 percent. For the Bank of Japan to succeed, achieving 2 percent inflation hinged on the attitude and expectations of the Japanese people. The road to the destination of 2 percent inflation in Japan was colored by the Bank of Japan's increasing share of the JGB market, which had lagged since 2008 relative to domestic banks' share (Figure 6.3 on page 193). In Japan, too, a confidence breakdown in JGBs may be driven by the Bank of Japan's using JGBs as one of the tools to tighten policy when 2 percent inflation prevails. Given the Japanese deflation attitude, reaching that goal may take a long time.

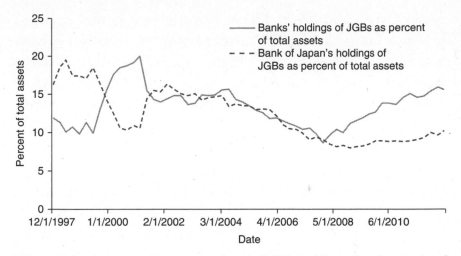

Figure 6.3 Japanese government bond (JGB) holdings by the Bank of Japan and domestic banks.

(*Source:* Bloomberg.)

U.S. Treasuries: Bond Vigilantes

Paul Krugman modeled how vigilantes would "attack" the U.S. government bond market. His conclusion was quite basic. A country with a floating currency would suffer an attack on its currency rather than on its bond market when loss of confidence occurred. The reason was that when bonds are issued in domestic rather than foreign currency, the loss of confidence feeds directly through currency depreciation, offsetting higher interest rates with improved terms of trade. Rising interest rates are not necessarily a "credit event" when debt is mostly controlled by domestic creditors. The opposite is true when debt is issued in foreign currency. The latter is the argument for the balance sheet approach. A country's aggregate balance sheet is then affected by four risk factors: (1) maturity mismatch, (2) currency mismatch, (3) capital structure, and (4) solvency. Each of these factors can trigger a balance of payments crisis during which vigilantes become visible through severe capital flight. This no longer seems to be the case thanks to central banks. Currency mismatch may not matter as much because many central banks attempt to influence currency valuations. Maturity mismatch and solvency are masked, too, by central bank asset purchase programs. What is perhaps missing here is the link between politics and growth. Austerity has structural benefits in terms of reforms, but piling too much austerity on a fragile economy may yield a situation of worsening deficits and growth that turns into a credit event attended by bond vigilantes. Too little austerity or commitment thereto may also lead to a credit event inspired by rating agency vigilantes. Have the bond vigilantes then become invisible? Or is the Krugman model correct and there is no reason for the vigilantes to exist? When debt is issued in domestic currency, Krugman's point is that a loss of confidence could be a benefit if that weakens the currency. So far, the confidence of domestic and foreign creditors in the Treasury market seems overwhelming. For the U.S. bond market to see the invisible vigilantes become visible, there is a greater political complexity at work. Figure 6.4 on page 195 shows that four major holders of U.S. Treasury debt, the Federal Reserve, China, OPEC (Organization of Petroleum Exporting Countries), and Japan, hold a combined 26 percent. Their shares have each steadily grown over the past decade despite the dollar's decline against the Chinese yuan and the Japanese yen. Thus, the real bond vigilantes are the official sector with a significant stake in the Treasury market. As the projected trend toward the right end of Figure 6.4 shows (*arrow*), the Federal Reserve is moving to overtake the three major foreign creditors. This may imply that the Federal Reserve has an "upper hand" as a bond vigilante. The difference is, however, that the growing size of the Federal Reserve's balance sheet complicates its exit from unconventional monetary policy. As in Japan, confidence in the U.S. Treasury market could be more strongly influenced by the Federal Reserve's steering of its balance sheet. Here, too, the unwinding process may take a while.

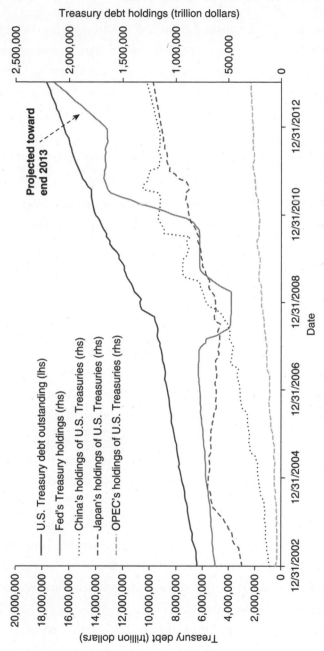

Figure 6.4 Treasury debt in the hands of different players. lhs, left-hand scale; OPEC, Organization of the Petroleum Exporting Countries; rhs, right-hand scale.

(*Sources:* U.S. Treasury Department, Federal Reserve, and Bloomberg.)

195

European Confidence: Common Bonds

In a stylized paper, the European Commission laid out the concept of "stability bonds." These bonds are pooled sovereign issuances aimed at sharing revenue flows and debt servicing. The credit rating depends on the credit quality of participating member states. There are several options: (1) several, not joint, guarantees for each specific contributor, (2) several, not joint, guarantees, but enhanced by seniority and collateral, and (3) joint and several guarantees. The AAA rating in (1) and (2) is greatly influenced by the potential downgrade of a large member. Under (3), even the European Commission acknowledged that an AAA rating might not be maintained if a limited number of AAA states were required to guarantee large liabilities of other lower-rated countries. Other conditions for stability bonds to work are a successful trade-off of relinquishing market discipline for fiscal discipline and the scope of monetary authority backing.

The valuation of stability bonds has seen empirical "estimates." The main assumption used is that common bonds should have a credit and liquidity premium similar to that of German government bonds ("Bunds"). Methods vary, but a simple weighted average of core Economic and Monetary Union (EMU) interest rates suggests a 1.5 percent premium on top of German Bunds. Others (Assmann, J.P. Morgan) use fiscal variables (multiplier, spending as percent of gross domestic product [GDP]) as input into regressions to derive a premium of about 60 basis points. Some (Morgan Stanley) have used Treasury rates as a comparable liquid common type bond by adjusting the Treasury yield for a currency premium. This method yields a 40- to 60-basis-point premium above comparable U.S. Treasury rates. Perhaps an easier approach is to just look at "proxy" common bonds such as the ones issued by the European Financial Stability Fund (EFSF) and the European Investment Bank (EIB). Taking the average yields of EFSF bonds suggests a premium of about 1 percent. These "proxy common bonds" (EFSF/EIB) are joint but not several, something that is likely to be a feature of a common bond, considering the political hurdles in Europe facing full common bond issuance.

Another new type of bond that was introduced was called "Elite bonds," issued by the standing AAA European countries. The Elite bond would provide a method for enforcing strict budget rules and allow the AAA countries to use their creditworthiness to provide aid to some peripheral countries. Methods show that by using GDP weights, the average Elite 10-year bond rate would be about 80 basis points above German Bunds. The diversity in risk premium difference (90–150 basis points) between Elite and stability bonds perhaps demonstrates wide outcomes as to how the EMU may ultimately evolve (a core group vs. EMU-17).

Another type of "safe bond" was proposed by the wiseman from Germany. The main idea is a redemption fund that pools the debt of countries exceeding 60 percent of GDP. Each country would be obliged to follow a consolidation path and thereby autonomously redeem the transferred debt over a period of 20 to 25 years. The redemption fund would issue Safe Bonds and use the proceeds to cover the financing of outstanding bond redemptions and new borrowing. The Safe Bonds would back the risk of existing bonds in the redemption fund, and so its risk premium over Bunds should presumably be wide.

The final idea for a common bond is the "blue-red bond" published by the Bruegel Institute in May 2010, which was later refined in a proposal by the European Commission. European countries would divide their total outstanding sovereign debt into two parts. The first part was to be pooled as "blue bonds" with senior status, for up to 60 percent of EMU's debt-to-GDP ratio. These bonds had to be jointly and severally guaranteed by participating countries. All debt beyond the 60 percent threshold was to be issued as "red bonds," which would have junior status. The blue bond would be a liquid and "safe" asset on the level of U.S. Treasury bonds. The idea was that the blue bonds would help the rise of the euro as a major reserve currency. It would enable the entire euro area to borrow part of the sovereign debt at interest rates comparable to those of German Bunds. The purpose of the red bonds was to enforce fiscal discipline on countries. Issuing red bonds would make borrowing more expensive and would impose market discipline in case a country lacked a credible fiscal policy. The European Commission sought to have red bonds kept mostly out of the European banking system to avoid the sovereign-bank loop. In addition, red bonds would be designed so that a planned orderly default mechanism could function in the euro area. The blue bond would be the "super safe" eurobond that would have no or limited default risk. The red bond was to take a majority share of sovereign risk and would be subject to PSI.

So what do stability, Elite, Safe, and blue-red bonds mean for the future government bond market in Europe? The discussion of common bonds still points to a joint but not several version. This may imply that "interest rate convergence," which went rather quickly in the 1990s ahead of the EMU, may take much longer in the future. The reason is that treaty changes with stricter fiscal rules are better suited for a smaller than a bigger group of EMU countries. As such, using an EMU GDP-weighted yield as a proxy for the common bond in Figure 6.5 and

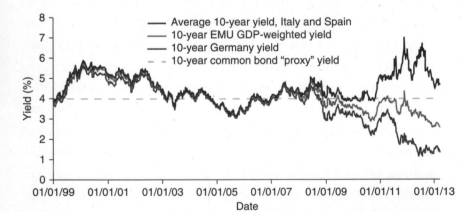

Figure 6.5 Common bonds in Europe. Economic and Monetary Union (EMU) gross domestic product (GDP)-weighted yield = GDP weight of each EMU country *10-year yield.

(*Source:* Bloomberg.)

comparing that with 10-year interest rates of Italy, Spain, and Germany from 1999 to 2012, there remain significant differences. The differences signify economic diversion, but also political division about the final end point of a full monetary union.

Theory of Debt Maturity Extensions

There are three ways of lowering the debt-to-GDP ratio: through (1) a "fiscal cut" with lower government spending, higher taxes, or both; (2) negative real rates; and (3) a sovereign rating downgrade. A consistent negative real interest rate is what Carmen Reinhart has described as financial repression through statutory means such as interest rate caps, bond floor prices, and tax incentives for deposits or quantitative easing. Both a fiscal and a real rate cut are backloaded measures, leading to stealth liquidation of debt over time. A rating cut can have a positive or negative immediate effect on the debt-to-GDP ratio. In "normal" times, monetary policy's goal is to stabilize inflation and fiscal policy to stabilize debt. Some Fed researchers (e.g., Woodford) have suggested that monetary policy plays an "active" role and fiscal policy a "passive" role. The roles tend to switch during a crisis. That is when monetary policy becomes unconventional while fiscal policy expands via automatic stabilizers and stimulus.

An abstract theory named fiscal theory of the price level (FTPL) argues that when that switch happens, fiscal, not monetary, policy has a direct impact on inflation. Passive monetary policy means setting no limits on inflation by allowing the real interest rate to be well below the level of real GDP. Especially when (long) interest rates are "pegged," the average duration of debt can extend, allowing the debt-to-GDP ratio to infinitely expand. As that occurs, the link between debt and inflation is determined by bond prices, which in turn can influence inflation expectations. The bottom line is that debt and inflation can move in tandem. Whether you believe Fisher, Richard Koo, Keynes, or even Ludwig von Mises, too much debt has a destructive effect on production and growth and thereby leads to deflation, not inflation. The FTPL has a point, however, that large amounts of debt entice monetary policy to be "passive" by allowing higher inflation to facilitate deleveraging. There is an overlap here with financial repression, which suggests that persistent negative real rates provide stealth liquidation of debt. It has appeared from the 2008 crisis that major central banks react asymmetrically, with drastic easing when inflation expectations fall but not so much when inflation rises. As the debt-to-GDP ratio is large and markets can threaten governments with higher interest rates to reach primary surplus, the central bank "facilitates" by keeping the zero bound and lower long-term government bond yields and extending the average duration of outstanding debt.

A New York Federal Reserve simulation showed that if the FTPL holds, then when short- and long-term interest rates are pegged, a switch from monetary to fiscal stimulus may prevent a deflationary spiral. A big assumption is that expectations are rational thanks to "effective" communication by monetary and fiscal policymakers. A caveat is that as central banks take on more bonds on their balance sheets, by the time the bonds mature, the central banks are collecting vast amounts of money from governments. Private savings have to offset that somehow, and in the absence of those, debt maturities extensions may occur more often. Issuance of 100-year-maturity debt at low or pegged rates may not be unrealistic for some of the major bond markets in the future (it is currently issued only in Mexico). FTPL suggests that bond prices become more sensitive to inflation expectations. Shifting the maturity of the public debt portfolio can influence future consumption decisions as well as inflation expectations. The theory says that the longer the maturity of the debt outstanding, the further out the risk of near default and the burden of the debt. That creates room for private investment and growth and thereby the possibility of higher inflation. Inflation has been extensively studied, but sometimes it can get momentum in a single moment. Such was the case in the United States when Arthur Burns, then chairman of the Federal Reserve, eased interest rates ahead of the 1972 presidential elections.

Arthur Burns's Moments

The exchange between Federal Reserve chairman Bernanke and Senator Schumer during the Humphrey-Hawkins testimony in July 2012 was by any measure historic. Schumer applauded Bernanke for being prudent about addressing fiscal discipline. Moreover, Schumer, given the political reality of the 2012 election year, strongly believed that the Fed was the "only game in town" to handle a dismal economy. As the risk of inflation in the United States was relatively low in 2012 to 2013 and the unemployment rate remained "sticky" at 7.5 to 8 percent, Schumer pushed Bernanke toward more action by saying: "Get to work, Mr. Chairman." In 1972, then Fed chairman Arthur Burns had had a similar experience when Nixon pushed him for monetary stimulus ahead of the presidential elections. That turned out to be a pivotal moment for what evolved into a decade of high inflation in the United States. Empirical studies of Federal Reserve behavior before presidential elections have not uncovered a general political monetary cycle, but such things can happen if the chairman and president share party allegiance. The transcripts from that time point to a Schumer-like persuasion, where Nixon in a private meeting told Burns: "You can lead 'em [the Federal Open Market Committee]. Just kick 'em in the rump a little."

There are always historical parallels. In 1970 to 1972, like today, the Fed viewed the economy as having an unusual, unexplainable way of functioning where high unemployment and inflation coexisted. Burns believed that monetary policy was not effective in combatting inflation, much like today, when Bernanke views it as not a panacea for fiscal policy. In 1971, real GDP growth stood at 2.5 to 3 percent, unemployment at 6 percent, and inflation near 3 percent when Burns was persuaded into monetary easing. He did so by cutting fed funds, increasing M1 and M2 to boost real GDP (+7.2 percent by quarter 4 of 1972), and nudging the unemployment rate down by 0.5 percent right before the elections. Today somewhat similar economic conditions exist. There are difficult political choices that must be made to properly address "fiscal cliffs." These choices have changed investors' perceptions of what is acceptable and what is not. Negative real yields are now part of the daily functioning of most developed inflation-linked bond markets. Negative real yields present a cost that is equivocally seen as higher than the cost of holding cash or the cost of realized inflation. What they reflect is expectations of much higher inflation sometime down the line in the future.

There are two schools of thought related to inflation: momentum and rational expectations. The momentum view says that the underlying inflation barely responds to monetary or fiscal policy. This is because it has left a "legacy" embedded in expectations, creating a momentum for extrapolating past inflation rates to the future. The alternative view is that people have "rational expectations" and strike wage and price bargains when it appears that current monetary and fiscal policy actions will be only temporary. Inflation therefore has a momentum of its own, imparted by persistent deficits and monetary expansion. Under the momentum view, inflation (or deflation) remains stubborn, but the rational expectations view suggests that inflation could suddenly change or stop if a policy regime shift were to take place. The speed of change in inflation is known as "inflation momentum." This is based on the definition of inflation as being a continuous change in prices. Historically, momentum in core inflation in the United States today as measured by the difference between shorter and longer moving averages is similar to that in the periods 1957 to 1966 and 1998 to 2007. Each saw an episode of relative calm in markets, economies, and politics. A distinct difference, however, is that the period from 1957 to 1966 was under a fixed exchange rate mechanism, Bretton Woods I. From 1998 to 2007, however, exchange rate fluctuations were modest; some academics such as Michael P. Dooley, David Folkerts-Landau and Peter Garber attributed this to the Bretton Woods II system. Perhaps a stronger argument is that each period did not experience a financial crisis but did see a war buildup (Vietnam, Iraq-Afghanistan).

To guess where inflation is going in the future is not an easy task. History, however, can help to a degree by, for example, comparing two episodes. It is notable that the momentum in Consumer Price Index (CPI) inflation—measured by the difference between the 1-year and 3-month moving average of the CPI—was very low ahead of a period of high inflation. That is to say that when looking at CPI history since World War II, as Figure 6.6 shows, pre–World War II inflation and momentum were far more volatile. What can be said, too, from Figure 6.6 is that monetary policy became ultra loose in both periods. In addition, as the "Arthur Burns moment" may suggest, there was greater willingness on the part of global central banks to engage in

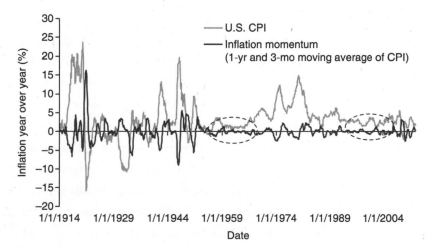

Figure 6.6 U.S. Consumer Price Index (CPI) and momentum.
(*Source:* Bloomberg.)

an aggressive cycle of monetary easing. Inflation momentum, aside from its basket weights technicalities, has steadily been increasing in the United States, the United Kingdom, and other developed countries. There is an element of "bad" inflation, such as higher food and energy prices, partly as a result of a weaker dollar because of easy Fed policy. There is also technical inflation because of fiscal austerity, like value-added taxes, consumption taxes, and utility hikes that drive up the CPI index. Real yields are negative across the maturity spectrum, a phenomenon that suggests that accelerating inflation momentum may drive inflation expectations toward higher realized inflation over time.

Measures of Debt Risks and Structural Trends

When judging debt on its risk-free character, one of the basic places to start is by looking at its underlying credit fundamentals. The IMF publishes such an overview in its Fiscal Monitor Report. Table 6.1 shows the major sovereign debt issuers and their vulnerabilities, measured by financing needs, external funding, and entitlement spending. From this overview, most sovereigns are vulnerable, with the exception of the Scandinavian countries, Australia, and New Zealand. They form "rings of fire," borrowing the analogy from PIMCO's Bill Gross and Johnny Cash. The rising debt-to-GDP ratios as well as negative primary balances present a fiscal gap that could become uncontrollable. As shown in Chapters 1 and 4, to stabilize the debt-to-GDP ratio relative to primary balances, nominal interest rates in many countries actually need to be negative. However, negative interest rates would be rejected by investors as an appropriate return, and with immediate fiscal consolidation put off except in a few European countries (Greece and Portugal), risk-free rates should be much higher. It is relevant for investors to understand that these risk metrics are dynamic because debt and GDP fluctuate in real time.

Table 6.1 Advanced Economies: Structural Fiscal Indicators
(Percent of GDP, Except Where Otherwise Indicated)

	Pension Spending Change, 2011–30	Health-care Spending Change, 2011–30	Gross Financing Needs, 2012–14	Debt-to-Average Maturity, 2012	Projected Interest Rate Growth Differential, 2012–17 (Percent)	Projected Overall Balance, 2012–17	Nonresident Holding of General Government Debt, 2012 (Percent of Total)	Debt to GDP Projection, 2012–17
Australia	0.8	2.1	5.3	5.3	-0.9	-0.6	51.2	24.9
Canada	1.9	2.0	16.5	17.2	0.0	-2.0	20.9	83.4
France	0.1	1.5	18.5	13.0	0.0	-2.4	64.1	90.6
Germany	1.1	0.9	8.5	12.9	-0.1	-0.2	61.7	78.5
Italy	-1.6	0.6	30.1	19.1	3.0	-1.6	35.2	125.2
Japan	-0.2	1.0	59.4	39.1	-0.5	-7.4	7.5	245.7
New Zealand	2.3	3.0	9.0	8.4	0.1	-1.1	—	36.8
Spain	0.5	1.6	22.6	15.8	2.9	-4.5	28.0	98.5
Sweden	-1.0	0.4	4.7	6.8	-1.2	1.0	45.8	31.6
United Kingdom	0.4	3.3	15.1	6.2	-0.7	-5.0	31.1	94.0
United States	1.7	5.1	26.3	20.0	-1.4	-5.8	30.2	112.5
Average	1.1	3.0	24.7	18.7	-0.7	-3.8	33.5	112.8
G-7	0.9	3.2	28.7	20.9	-0.7	-4.8	31.8	128.2
G-20 advanced	1.1	3.2	26.8	19.8	-0.8	-4.4	32.1	120.4

(*Sources:* Bloomberg L.P.; national authorities; Haver Analytics; Organisation for Economic Co-operation and Development; OECD.Stat; Joint External Debt Hub; and IMF staff estimates and projections.)

Another key secular risk is population growth. In the 2010 to 2012 mortality report, the United Nations projected falling growth in population across the world. By the year 2045, the United States, Asia, and Europe will have negative population growth of about half a percent annually. The implication is that population growth is directly connected to productivity, and, added together, they serve as a proxy for potential GDP. Falling population growth confirms that a further decline in potential GDP may be likely. That could have an impact on asset returns. The most important factor is life expectancy, which has shifted to 87 years on average for the developed countries such as the United States, the United Kingdom, and Japan, according to the United Nations population division. This implies that for a population that is shrinking and has a greater share of elderly people, the case of Japan remains a proxy for how sovereign risk has to be controlled. Japan's aging population, which is well advanced, is a pressing matter for Japan's debt-to-GDP ratio. Given that potential output falls as the population ages, the amount of resources available shrinks, which means that the burden falls on the Japanese central bank to monetize debt in order to retire the outstanding debt in an "orderly" manner. This doesn't go without a tax of some sort, possibly higher inflation through currency devaluation. As that happens, real interest rates should rise, as they reflect a higher inflation risk. It is notable from Figure 6.7 on page 207 that forward real interest rates implied from the TIPS and inflation swap markets point to a sharper rise in the future as population declines. Although these are "projections" derived from forward interest rates, they imply a risk premium of future GDP growth that because of a smaller population is no longer able to generate past levels of production.

History of Sovereign Bond Yields

Over the centuries, interest rates in major economies have always had a close correlation with one another. The levels of GDP, inflation, and population growth have not been too dissimilar in those countries.

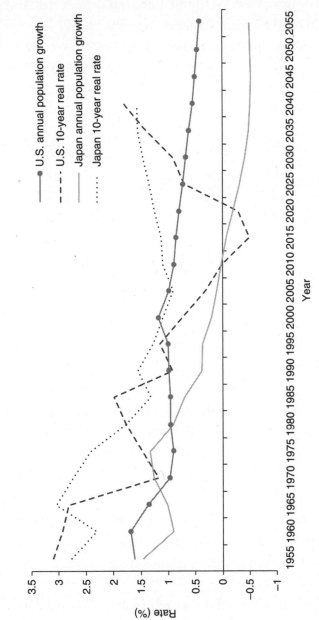

Figure 6.7 Population and interest rates. Ten-year rates after 2012 are derived from forward rates.

(*Source:* United Nations Population Division, Bloomberg.)

This explains to a degree the close relationship between interest rates as they present the sum of real GDP, inflation, and default risk. In Figure 6.8 on page 209, taken from Bank of America Merrill Lynch's "The Longest Pictures" publication, history since 1790 shows how long-term interest rates follow economic cycles. In the next subsections, two specific cases are discussed.

Italy

Italy has been known for its debt issuance and its love for monetization. There are three distinct phases in Italian monetary policy history. Phase I was in the 1970s, when Italy pursued a policy of debt monetization whereby the central bank was obligated by law to buy unsold bonds at Italian Treasury auctions. There was a unique relationship between the Treasury and the central bank through a so-called overdraft account that the Treasury held at the bank. The Treasury created an excess monetary base by issuing debt in the primary market, and the central bank would "spend" the excess base in the overdraft account by buying the unsold bonds. Because the auctions were noncompetitive, the Italian Treasury was in a position to take advantage of the relationship it had with the central bank. The Treasury would set a minimum auction price at which the central bank would mop up the unsold residual of the auction. The price the Treasury set for the central bank was typically higher than that in the secondary market and was passed on as a subsidy to the government. Because central bank policy was subordinated, the creation of excess money and resulting rising inflation were met with administrative measures by requiring commercial banks to invest a fraction of their deposits in long-term bonds to keep interest rates low.

Financial repression certainly existed in Italy. That did not keep interest rates from spiking in the mid to late 1970s, well above interest rates in other countries. By 1981, phase II had started via a "monetary

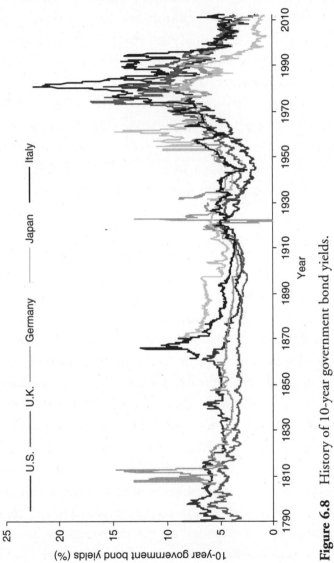

Figure 6.8 History of 10-year government bond yields.
(*Source:* Merrill Lynch.)

reform" that released the central bank from its obligation to buy unsold debt. By making auctions more competitive, the "hope" was to separate monetary from fiscal policy and thereby attempt to reduce the size of the Treasury's overdraft account. The monetary reforms were only gradually ratified by new laws as Italian policymakers put capital controls in place during Italian lira depreciations. The sizable overdraft account (three times the average in Europe) kept monetary policy dependent on the Italian Treasury's debt monetization expectations. This kept Italian bond yields high well into the 1990s. The 2010 to 2011 European debt crisis showed that Italian bond yields "mean reverted" halfway to their long-run average of 14 percent, shown by Figure 6.8. Bond yield history may not always prove right in terms of what could happen next, but in the words of Mark Twain, "History does not repeat itself, but it does rhyme."

The Netherlands

When the Netherlands won the 80-year war (1568–1648) against Spain, one of the first government bond markets was formed. Part of the development of Dutch bonds was that as the Netherlands became an economic power, Amsterdam became a financial trade center. As part of a flourishing trade, the Dutch East India Company was founded in 1602 and the Dutch West India Company in 1621. On the Amsterdam Exchange, shares of the Dutch East India Company and the Dutch West India Company were actively traded. In addition to tulip forward agreements, government bonds were traded. Dutch bonds were in the form of annuities issued by local governments, such as provinces and towns. This is how state financing was developed. The Dutch government would pledge its revenues against the annuities issued. These annuities were guaranteed by the general credit of the Dutch state. Dutch bonds promised fixed annual coupon payments into the indefinite future. These are known as consoler perpetuities. Because they offered an indefinite flow of interest payments, the Dutch consoles became popular among wealthy families, who would buy them with the idea that they could live comfortably off the income for generations. The success of the Dutch financial system and market financing led to its inevitable adoption by other countries, including the United States and the United Kingdom. Although marketable in principle, each of the Dutch bonds as well as Dutch tulip futures represented a unique contract. In their detailed work *The History of Interest Rates*, Homer and Sylla describe how interest rate contracts played a key role in ancient times:

> The supra secular patterns of minimum interest rates provided by this method of analysis had a good deal of similarity. In all three cases interest rates seemed to decline from earliest history until a period of late commercial development, and later to advance during the final centuries of political breakdown (p. 64).

This description of how interest rates behave in cycles stands today. Taken from their book, Figure 6.9 on page 212 shows that in ancient Rome and Greece, trends in interest rates were at average levels of 4 to 10 percent. That is not that different from where Greek and Italian bond yields have traded from the middle of the 1990s until today. Furthermore, Homer and Sylla's research in medieval Europe has found ranges for interest rates charged on loans, deposits, and annuities to be similar, around 4 to 12 percent.

Final Words: End of the Risk-Free Rate?

This book has taken a journey on the concept of the risk-free rate and how it has changed. *By no means is the purpose of this book to argue that bonds are no longer prudent or unsuitable investments.* Chapter 5, for example, presented alternatives in fixed income, and more could be named, such as supra-sovereign, quasi-agency, convertible, and catastrophe bonds. These asset classes have unique risk-return profiles and

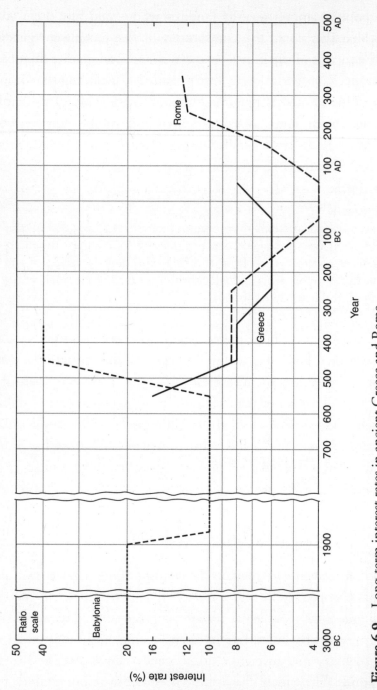

Figure 6.9 Long-term interest rates in ancient Greece and Rome.

(*Source:* Sydney Homer and Richard Sylla, *The History of Interest Rates*, 4th ed. [Hoboken, NJ: Wiley Finance, 2005].)

may be attractive, too, obviously depending on valuation and risks. This book is not an attempt to replicate the kind of book that Carmen Reinhart and Ken Rogoff have written about sovereign debt crises through time. Their work *This Time Is Different* comes highly recommended as a way to understand the intricacies of sovereign debt crises. Rather, this book spends time on discussing why risk premiums and the risk-free rate could be different going forward. More so, it tries to answer the central question, what if there is truly an end to the risk-free rate, the benchmark that is widely used in our financial system? If one were to take history again for granted, then Figure 6.10 argues that the instrument most widely used as the risk-free rate—the 3-month Treasury bill—at 0.001 percent should eventually go higher. Even the historical average of 3.7 percent in Figure 6.10 may seem meaningless;

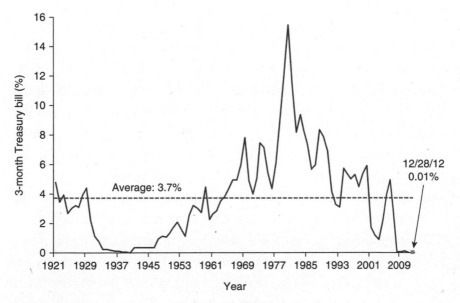

Figure 6.10 U.S. 3-month Treasury bill history.
(*Source:* Merrill Lynch.)

if short-term interest rates were to go to that level, it would likely have a material impact on financial and tangible assets.

There is the thesis that interest rates exhibit "mean reversion." That phenomenon underscores the idea of bubble management by central banks. The Vasicek model has attempted, as a stochastic investment model, to treat interest rates differently from other asset prices. The main assumption of the model is that interest rates cannot rise indefinitely. This is because at very high levels, they would hamper economic activity, prompting a decrease in interest rates. Similarly, interest rates cannot decrease below 0 percent. As a result, interest rates move in a limited range, showing a tendency to revert to a long-run value. Not to end on a quantitative note, but the models by Vasicek do have merit when it comes to the behavior of interest rates. In fact, an input is the risk-free money market rate as a risk-neutral measure, as part of Black's formula of forward bond prices, as well as Black-Scholes option pricing. The change of the risk-neutral assumption based on the analysis presented in this book hopefully challenges academia and market practitioners to recalibrate derivatives, the capital asset pricing model, and other models on which so much in finance is built. The risk-free rate may have ended, but bonds will always play an integral role in finance. History from the distant past to the present time has shown that without bond financing, much of societies, economies, politics, and markets cannot function. The timing of changes in interest rates is a puzzle in itself. As explained, the significant amounts of $6 to $7 trillion notional in government bonds that central banks hold in custody with an average maturity of 5 to 7 years, according to the Bank for International Settlements (BIS), pose a huge challenge for the future. The unwinding of that sum may revisit the up-and-down cycle of history in interest rates, as shown by Homer and Sylla. For bond investors, it means that the foundation of fixed income strategy always remains in place, no matter what level of interest rates prevails.

This investment foundation is rather simple:

- Seek steep, upward-sloping yield curves to earn carry, price, and roll-down return.
- Invest in positive real yielding assets, not negative yielding assets.
- Diversify among government, agency, covered, corporate, high-yield, inflation-linked, and mortgage bonds.
- Tread carefully when taking foreign exchange risk. Currency comes with volatility, and the implied carry is not the same as coupon interest or dividend income streams.
- Equity risk premium may look historically high, but to be successful in equity investing, it requires a prolific stock picker. Look at return on invested capital versus the weighted average cost of capital to find true value among companies.
- Understand market depth, liquidity, and capital flows and how these change; what the transaction costs are; and what regulations affect the structure of the marketplace.
- Continuously educate yourself on economic trends, politics, and social movements.
- Be a trader or a portfolio manager, but wear the hat of a policymaker to better understand what may come next.
- Develop a debt risk matrix with the help of data from IMF, Organisation for Economic Co-operation and Development, BIS, and World Bank sources.
- Become a profound central bank watcher to gauge the exit from unconventional policy. The websites of the Federal Reserve, Bank of England, European Central Bank, and Bank of Japan offer significant information transparency on policy and research. An investor has to make it a daily habit to read those websites.

- Look to establish a portfolio that is a combination of generally liquid means, exchange-traded funds, mutual funds, and individual securities.
- Do not believe the hype about *any* asset.

A Dutch saying is *en geen cent teveel!* The English translation is "not a penny too many." A penny is what perhaps will always be seen as risk free, but even a penny can be stolen or destroyed. In a zero or negative interest rate world, investors may want to seek pennies in front of the steamroller. There are, however, always alternatives to cash and pennies, even those that are seen as an equivalent risk. What has to be reconsidered is whether the risk-free rate is what it once resembled—a risk-free return at low or no cost. There is not a penny that is too many to assume that a risk-free return exists in an ever more risky, uncertain, and volatile global economy.

References

Chapter 1

Bank for International Settlements. *Quarterly Review*, September 2012.

Barro, Robert J. "Are Government Bonds Net Wealth?" *Journal of Political Economy* 82 (6), pp. 1095–1117, 1974.

Bullard, James. *Seven Faces of the Peril.* St. Louis Federal Reserve, 2010.

European Central Bank press conference, September 2012. Available at http://www.ecb.int/press/pressconf/2012/html/is120906.en.html.

European Central Bank press conference, October 2012. Available at http://www.ecb.int/press/pressconf/2012/html/is121004.en.html.

Fisher, Irving. *The Theory of Interest as Determined by Impatience to Spend Income and Opportunity to Invest it.* New York: Macmillan, 1930.

Friedman, Milton. "The Real Free Lunch: Markets and Private Property." Cato Policy Report, 1993.

International Monetary Fund. "IMF's World Economic Outlook." International Monetary Fund, Publication Services, P.O. Box 92780, Washington, DC 20090, October 2012.

Mehra, Rajnish, and Edward C. Prescott. "The Equity Premium: A Puzzle." *Journal of Monetary Economics* 15 (2), pp. 145–161, 1985.

Pigou, Arthur Cecil. "The Classic Stationary State." *Economic Journal* 53 (212), pp. 343–351, 1943.

Schmidt, Michael, CFA. "How Risk Free Is the Risk Free Rate of Return?" Investopedia, February 2009.

Vinals, Jose. "Government Bonds: No Longer a World Without Risk." International Monetary Fund, Washington, DC, 2011.

Chapter 2

Baker, Scott, Nick Bloom, and Steven Davis. Policy Uncertainty Index. Available at http://www.policyuncertainty.com.

Bank of England. Inflation Report, August 2012. Available at http://www.bankofeng land.co.uk/publications/Documents/inflationreport/ir12aug.pdf.

Bank of England. Statistics on monetary policy decisions. Available at http://www .bankofengland.co.uk/monetarypolicy/Pages/decisions.aspx.

Bartlett, Bruce. "How Romney Could End Quantitative Easing." *Financial Times*, A-List, October 16, 2012, http://blogs.ft.com/the-a-list/2012/10/16/how-romney -could-end-quantitative-easing/#axzz2O2askjfR.

De Grauwe, Paul. *The Governance of a Fragile Eurozone*. Brussels, Belgium: University of Leuven, Center for European Policy Studies, 2012.

Forbes, Kristin J. "The Big C, Identifying and Mitigating Contagion." Jackson Hole Economic Symposium, Jackson Hole, Wyoming, August 2012.

Friedman, Milton. "The Role of Monetary Policy." *American Economic Review* 58 (1), pp. 1–17, 1968.

Gordon, Robert. "Is U.S. Economic Growth Over? Faltering Innovation Confronts the Six Headwinds." Northwestern University, Department of Economics; National Bureau of Economic Research (NBER); Centre for Economic Policy Research (CEPR), London, U.K., 2012.

Greenspan, Alan. "Productivity." Federal Reserve, U.S. Department of Labor and American Enterprise Institute Conference, Washington, DC, 2002.

Krugman, Paul. "A Model of Balance of Payments Crisis." *Journal of Money, Banking and Credit* 11, pp. 311–325, 1979.

McGrattan, Ellen R., and Edward C. Prescott. "The Labor Productivity Puzzle." Working Paper No. 694. Minneapolis: Federal Reserve Bank of Minneapolis Research Department, 2012.

Okun, Arthur. *Potential GNP: Its Measurement and Significance*. Cowles Foundation, Yale University, New Haven, CT, 1962.

Organisation for Economic Co-operation and Development. OECD economic outlook annex tables. Available at http://www.oecd.org/eco/economicoutlook analysisandforecasts/economicoutlookannextables.htm.

Phelps, Edmund S. "Phillips Curves, Expectations of Inflation and Optimal Employment over Time." *Economica* 34 (3), pp. 254–281, 1967.

Phillips, A. W. "The Relationship Between Unemployment and the Rate of Change of Money Wages in the United Kingdom 1861–1957." *Economica* 25 (100), pp. 283–299, 1958.

Reinhart, Carmen. "Capital Flows to Latin America: Is There Evidence of Contagion Effects?" Washington, DC: Institute for International Economics, pp. 151–171, 1996.

———. "Two Hundred Years of Contagion." MPRA Working Paper No. 13229, 2002.

——— and Kenneth S. Rogoff. "The Forgotten History of Domestic Debt." Working Paper No. 13946. National Bureau of Economic Research. http://www.nber.org/papers/w13946.

Schineller, Lisa. "A Nonlinear Econometric Analysis of Capital Flight." Washington, DC: Federal Reserve Board, 1997.

Sheets, Nathan, and Robert Sockin. "Capital-Hours Ratio, Real GDP Per Capita." New York: Citigroup Research, 2012.

Yellen, Janet. "The Economic Outlook and Monetary Policy." New York: Federal Reserve, Money Marketeers of New York University, 2012.

———. "The US Economy: Prospects and a Puzzle Revisited." Speech given to the Money Marketeers of New York University, New York, 2007.

Chapter 3

Atkins, Ralph. Interview transcript: Lorenzo Bini Smaghi. *Financial Times*, May 25, 2011.

Baldacci, Emanuele, Sanjeev Gupta, and Carlos Mulas-Granados. "Restoring Debt Sustainability After Crises: Implications for the Fiscal Mix." Washington, DC: IMF, Working Paper, 2010.

Bank for International Settlements. "Report of the G-10 Working Group on Contractual Clauses," Basel, Switzerland, 2002.

Bradley & Gulati. "Collective Action Clauses for the Eurozone: An Empirical Analysis." Duke University Papers, 2011.

Congressional Budget Office. "2012 Long-Term Budget Outlook." Washington, DC.

Cox, Chris, and Bill Archer. "Why $16 Trillion Only Hints at the True U.S. Debt." *Wall Street Journal*, November 28, 2012.

Dalio, Ray. "An In-Depth Look at Deleveragings." Bridgewater, CT: Bridgewater Associates LP, 2012.

Eichengreen, Barry. "Restructuring Sovereign Debt." *Journal of Economic Perspectives* 17, pp. 75–98, 2003.

———, and Ashoka Mody. "Do Collective Action Clauses Raise Borrowing Costs?" *Economic Journal* 114, pp. 247–264, 2004.

————. "Would Collective Action Clauses Raise Borrowing Costs? An Update and Additional Results," 2000. Available at http://ideas.repec.org/p/cdl/ciders/1008.html.

Emons, Ben. "Collective Action Clauses; No Panacea for Sovereign Restructurings." Pacific Investment Management Company, Newport Beach, CA, 2012.

Feroli, James. "Ten Year Mirage." J.P. Morgan Research, New York, 2012.

McKinsey Global Institute. "Debt and Deleveraging: Uneven Progress on the Path to Growth." McKinsey & Company, London, U.K., 2012.

Richards, Anthony. "Do Collective Action Clauses Influence Bond Yields? New Evidence from Emerging Markets." Reserve Bank of Australia Research Working Paper No. 2003-02, Sydney, Australia, March 2003.

Rosa, Carlo. "How Unconventional Are Large Scale Asset Purchases? The Impact of Monetary Policy on Asset Prices." New York: New York Federal Reserve, Staff Report No. 560, 2012.

Roubini, Nouriel. "Bail-ins, Bailouts, Burden Sharing and Private Sector Involvement in Crisis Resolution: The G-7 Framework and Some Suggestions." Stern School of Business, New York University, New York, 2001.

Sahay, Ratna. "A Survey of Experiences with Emerging Market Sovereign Debt Restructurings." IMF Working Paper, 2012.

Chapter 4

Arslanalp, Serkan, and Takahiro Tsuda. "Tracking Global Demand for Advanced Economy Sovereign Debt." IMF Working Paper No. 284, 2012.

Bernanke, Ben. "The Economic Recovery and Economic Policy." Speech given at the New York Economic Club. New York: New York Federal Reserve, 2012.

Damodaran, Aswath. "Country Risk Premiums, 2012." Available at http://people.stern.nyu.edu/adamodar/pc/datasets/ctrypremJune2012.xls.

Dornbusch, Rudiger. "Expectations and Exchange Rate Dynamics." *Journal of Political Economy* 84 (6), pp. 1161–1176, 1976.

Euromoney. Country Risk Index: "ECR." Available at http://www.euromoneycountryrisk.com.

Federal Open Market Committee. Statement, December 12, 2012. Available at http://www.federalreserve.gov/newsevents/press/monetary/20121212a.htm.

Graham, Benjamin. *Security Analysis.* New York: McGraw-Hill, 1934.

Keynes, John Maynard. *General Theory of Employment, Interest and Money.* London: Palgrave MacMillan, 1936.

Reinhart, Carmen. "The Return of Financial Repression." Banque de France, Paris, France. *Financial Stability Review* 16, 2012.

Stein, Jeremy, and Samuel G. Hanson. "Monetary Policy and Long Term Real Rates." Washington, DC. Federal Reserve Board, 2012.

Tobin, James. "Asset Markets and the Cost of Capital. Economic Progress, Private Values and Public Policy." Amsterdam: North-Holland, 1977.

Yellen, Janet. "Perspectives on Monetary Policy." Speech given at the Boston Economic Club Dinner, Boston, 2012.

Chapter 5

Canadian Mortgage Housing Corporation. Covered Bond Framework, 2012. Available at http://www.cmhc.ca/en/hoficlincl/cacobo/index.cfm.

Deutsche Bank Research. "Covered Bond Outlook 2012." New York, 2012.

Dick-Nielsen, Jens, Jacob Gyntelberg, and Thomas Sangill. "Liquidity in Government Versus Covered Bond Markets." Basel, Switzerland: Bank for International Settlements, Working Paper No. 392, 2012.

Duffie, Darrel. "The Relation Between Treasury Yields and Corporate Bond Yield Spreads." *Journal of Finance* 54, pp. 2225–2241, 1998.

European Commission. Working Paper of the Commission Services on the Treatment of Covered Bonds, European Commission, Brussels, Belgium, 2012.

Gonzalez-Rozada, Martin, and Eduardo Yeyati. "Global Factors and Emerging Market Spreads." *Economic Journal*, 118, pp. 1917–1936, 2008.

Gourinchas, Pierre-Olivier, and Olivier Jeanne. "Global Safe Assets." Basel, Switzerland: Bank for International Settlements, Working Paper No. 399, 2012.

Ibbotson, Roger. *The Equity Risk Premium*. New Haven, CT: Yale School of Management, 2000.

International Monetary Fund. "IMF 2012 Financial Stability Report." Washington, DC, 2012.

Longstaff, Frank, and Erik Schwartz. "A Simple Approach to Valuing Risky Fixed and Floating Rate Debt." *Journal of Finance* 50, pp. 789–820, 1995.

Miyajima, Ken, Madhusudan Mohanty, and Tracy Chan. "Emerging Market Local Currency Bonds: Diversification and Stability." Basel, Switzerland: Bank for International Settlements, Working Paper No. 391, 2012.

Shiller, Robert. *Irrational Exuberance*, 2nd ed. Princeton, NJ: Princeton University Press, 2005.

Chapter 6

Bank of America Merrill Lynch. "The Longest Pictures." Bank of America Research, New York, 2012.

Bernanke, Ben. "Humprey Hawkins Testimony Before Congress," Washington, DC, 2012.

European Commission. "Green Paper on Feasibility of Introducing Stability Bonds." Brussels, Belgium: European Commission, 2011.

Dooley, Michael P., David Folkerts-Landau, and Peter Garber. "An Essay on the Revised Bretton Wood System." National Bureau of Economic Research, Working Paper No. 9971, 2003.

Greenspan, Alan. "Opening Remarks." Jackson Hole Economic Symposium, Jackson Hole, Wyoming, 2005.

Gross, William Hunt. "The Ring of Fire. Investment Outlook." Pacific Investment Management Company, Newport Beach, California, 2010.

Homer, Sydney, and Richard Sylla. *The History of Interest Rates*, 4th ed. Hoboken, NJ: Wiley Finance, 2005.

International Monetary Fund. "IMF Financial Stability Report." Washington, DC: IMF, 2012.

Krugman, Paul. "The Simple Analytics of Invisible Bond Vigilantes." *New York Times*, November 9, 2012.

United Nations. "United Nations Mortality Report, 2010–2012." New York.

Vasicek, Oldrich. "An Equilibrium Characterization of the Term Structure." *Journal of Financial Economics* 5, pp. 177–188, 1977.

von Weiszacker, Jakob, and Jacques Delpla. "The Blue Bond Proposal." Bruegel Institute, Brussels, Belgium, 2010.

Waikei, Raphael Lam, and Kiichi Tokuoka. "Assessing the Risks of the Japanese Government Bond (JGBs) Market." Washington, DC: IMF Working Paper No. 292, 2011.

Woodford, Michael. *Public Debt and the Price Level.* Princeton, NJ: Princeton University Press, 1998.

Index

225

About the Author

Ben Emons is a Senior Vice President and Global Portfolio Manager at Pacific Investment Management Company in Newport Beach, California. Prior to joining PIMCO, he worked as a portfolio manager at Nuveen Investments in Los Angeles and as a Senior Fixed Income strategist and derivatives specialist at ABN AMRO Bank in Amsterdam, the Netherlands, and London, the United Kingdom. He has 19 years of professional experience in financial markets. He is the author of *The Financial Domino Effect* and frequently writes about topics in macroeconomics, central banks, and sovereign-covered bond markets on PIMCO's website (www.pimco.com). He also writes a monthly column in the *Dutch Financial Times—Het Financieele Dagblad*—on a broad range of European topics. In addition, he writes about topics from *The Financial Domino Effect* on the McGraw-Hill Business Blog. He has a master's degree in International Finance and Monetary Economics from the University of Amsterdam and a Master's of Business Administration from the University of Southern California.